GRADE
4

Common Core Language

D0745292

Table of Contents

Introduction

What Is the Common Core?

The Common Core State Standards are an initiative by states to set shared, consistent, and clear criteria for what students are expected to learn. This helps teachers and parents know what they need to do to help students. The standards are designed to be rigorous and pertinent to the real world. They reflect the knowledge and skills that young people need for success in college and careers.

If you teach in a state that has joined the Common Core State Standards Initiative, then you are required to incorporate these standards into your lesson plans. Students need targeted practice in order to meet grade-level standards and expectations, and thereby be promoted to the next grade.

What Does the Common Core Say About Language Standards?

In order for students to be college- and career-ready in language, they must gain control over many conventions of standard English grammar, usage, and mechanics, as well as learn other ways to use language to convey meaning effectively.

Research shows that it is effective to use students' writing as a tool to integrate grammar practice. However, it is often hard to find a suitable context in which to teach such specific grade-level standards. Some students will need additional, explicit practice of certain skills. The mini-lessons and practice pages in this book will help them get the practice they need so they can apply the required skills during independent writing and on standardized assessments.

Students must also be proficient in vocabulary acquisition skills. This means being able to determine or clarify the meaning of grade-appropriate words. It also means being able to appreciate that words have nonliteral meanings, shades of meaning, and relationships to other words. These skills will enable students to read and comprehend rigorous informational texts and complex literary texts.

The Common Core State Standards state that the "inclusion of Language standards in their own strand should not be taken as an indication that skills related to conventions, effective language use, and vocabulary are unimportant to reading, writing, speaking, and listening; indeed, they are inseparable from such contexts."

Using This Book

Mini-Lessons and Practice Pages

Each grade-level volume in this series addresses all of the Language standards for that grade. For each standard, three types of resources are provided that scaffold students using a gradual release model.

Based on your observations of students' language in writing and in collaborative conversations, choose mini-lessons that address their needs. The mini-lessons can be used during your literacy and writing block. Then use the practice pages to reinforce skills.

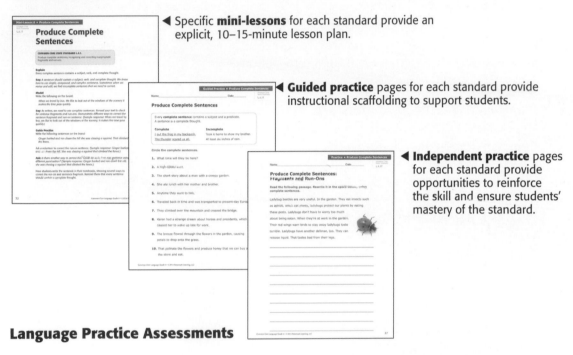

◄ Specific **mini-lessons** for each standard provide an explicit, 10–15-minute lesson plan.

◄ **Guided practice** pages for each standard provide instructional scaffolding to support students.

◄ **Independent practice** pages for each standard provide opportunities to reinforce the skill and ensure students' mastery of the standard.

Language Practice Assessments

Easy-to-use, flexible practice assessments for both Conventions and Vocabulary standards are provided in the last section of the book. The self-contained 2-page assessments cover skills in a reading passage format and have multiple choice answers.

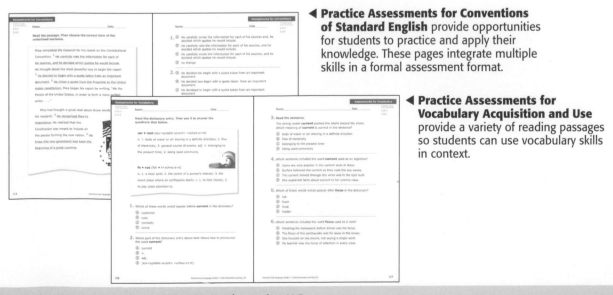

◄ **Practice Assessments for Conventions of Standard English** provide opportunities for students to practice and apply their knowledge. These pages integrate multiple skills in a formal assessment format.

◄ **Practice Assessments for Vocabulary Acquisition and Use** provide a variety of reading passages so students can use vocabulary skills in context.

Lesson Plan Teacher Worksheet
Conventions of Standard English and Knowledge of Language

The lessons in this section are organized in the same order as the Common Core Language Standards for conventions. Each mini-lesson provides specific, explicit instruction for a Language standard and is followed by multiple practice pages. Use the following chart to track the standards students have practiced. You may wish to revisit mini-lesson and practice pages a second time for spiral review.

Common Core State Standard	Mini-Lessons and Practice	Page	Complete (✓)	Review (✓)
L.4.1a	Mini-Lesson 1: Relative Pronouns and Relative Adverbs	6		
	Practice Pages: Relative Pronouns	7		
	Practice Pages: Relative Adverbs	9		
L.4.1b	Mini-Lesson 2: Progressive Tenses	12		
	Practice Pages: Past Progressive	13		
	Practice Pages: Present Progressive	15		
	Practice Pages: Future Progressive	17		
L.4.1c	Mini-Lesson 3: Modal Auxiliaries	20		
	Practice Pages: Modal Auxiliaries	21		
L.4.1d	Mini-Lesson 4: Order Adjectives	24		
	Practice Pages: Order Adjectives	25		
L.4.1e	Mini-Lesson 5: Form and Use Prepositional Phrases	28		
	Practice Pages: Form and Use Prepositional Phrases	29		

Conventions of Standard English and Knowledge of Language

Common Core State Standard	Mini-Lessons and Practice	Page	Complete (✓)	Review (✓)
L.4.1f	Mini-Lesson 6: Produce Complete Sentences	32		
	Practice Pages: Produce Complete Sentences	33		
L.4.1g	Mini-Lesson 7: Correctly Use Frequently Confused Words	38		
	Practice Pages: Correctly Use Frequently Confused Words	39		
L.4.2a	Mini-Lesson 8: Use Correct Capitalization	42		
	Practice Pages: Use Correct Capitalization	43		
L.4.2b	Mini-Lesson 9: Use Commas and Quotation Marks	46		
	Practice Pages: Use Commas and Quotation Marks	47		
	Practice Pages: Use Commas and Quotation Marks for Quotations	50		
L.4.2c	Mini-Lesson 10: Use a Comma in a Compound Sentence	54		
	Practice Pages: Use a Comma in a Compound Sentence	55		
L.4.2d	Mini-Lesson 11: Use Reference Materials to Spell	58		
	Practice Pages: Use Reference Materials to Spell	59		
L.4.3a	Mini-Lesson 12: Choose Words and Phrases to Convey Ideas Precisely	62		
	Practice Pages: Choose Words and Phrases to Convey Ideas Precisely	63		
L.4.3b	Mini-Lesson 13: Choose Punctuation for Effect	66		
	Practice Pages: Choose Punctuation for Effect	67		
L.4.3c	Mini-Lesson 14: Formal and Informal English	70		
	Practice Pages: Formal and Informal English	71		

COMMON CORE
STATE STANDARD
L.4.1a

Relative Pronouns and Relative Adverbs

> **COMMON CORE STATE STANDARD L.4.1a**
> Use relative pronouns (*who, whose, whom, which, that*) and relative adverbs (*where, when, why*).

Explain

Tell students that relative pronouns and relative adverbs introduce a dependent clause in a sentence and give more information about a word or phrase in the sentence.

Say: *A pronoun is a word that refers to a noun. A relative pronoun gives more information about a word or phrase in the sentence. Use the relative pronouns* who, whom, *and* whose *to refer to people, and* that *and* which *to refer to things.*

An adverb is a describing word. A relative adverb gives more information about a word or phrase in the sentence. The relative adverbs *where*, *when*, and *why* can take the place of a preposition plus the word *which*.

Model

Write these sentences on the board:

> *My sister, who is a year younger than I am, plays the flute.*
> *I remember the day when my brother graduated high school.*

Point out that *who* is a relative pronoun that gives more information about the sister. Point out that *when* is a relative adverb that gives more information about the day.

Guide Practice

Write these sentences on the board. Ask a volunteer to underline the relative pronoun or relative adverb in the first sentence.

1. *James, who is Tommy's school playmate, lives on a houseboat.* (who)
2. *The vase, which looks ordinary, is mom's favorite.* (which)
3. *She told me the reason why I received a bad grade on the term paper.* (why)

Ask: *Did you underline the relative pronouns or relative adverbs?*

Repeat the procedure with each sentence. Have the students find the relative pronoun or relative adverb in each sentence. Remind them that the relative pronouns *who*, *whom*, and *whose* refer to people and *that* and *which* refer to things. Relative adverbs *where*, *when*, and *why* can take the place of a preposition plus the word *which*.

Name_____ Date_____

Relative Pronouns

A **relative pronoun** links two clauses together by giving more information about a word or phrase in the sentence. The pronoun "relates" to the noun that it modifies. The relative pronouns are **who**, **whom**, **whose**, **that**, and **which**.

- The lamp <u>that</u> is on the table needs a new light bulb.
- The nurse, <u>who</u> started her shift at five in the morning, is tired.
- Giraffes, <u>which</u> are tall animals, can eat leaves from tall trees.

Choose the correct relative pronoun from the box that fits with each sentence. Write it on the line.

who	whom	whose	that	which

1. An astronaut is a person _____ travels into space.

2. He picked shoes _____ have buckles.

3. Josie received a bracelet, _____ was purple and black, for her birthday.

4. The novel, _____ author was known for writing children's books, was written for adults.

5. My teacher, _____ you have met before, will be there tonight.

COMMON CORE
STATE STANDARD
L.4.1a

Name_____ Date_____

Relative Pronouns

Read each sentence. Underline the relative pronoun and circle the word or phrase the relative pronoun describes.

1. The crab, which crawled slowly across the beach, was shaped like a horseshoe.

2. Mauri took her boot with a broken heel to a cobbler, who is a person who repairs shoes.

3. The delivery truck driver lost the package that I was expecting to receive today.

4. The rabbit, which was brown, burrowed into the ground to hide from the hot sun.

5. The teacher, whom I have been waiting for all morning, has finally arrived.

6. A plantain is a fruit that is similar to a banana.

7. The toddler, who was barely three years old, could recite the entire alphabet.

8. Carin looked up the meaning of the word *mechanical* in the dictionary, which is used to find the definitions of words.

9. The jury handed the envelope to the judge, who immediately opened it.

10. I have a classmate whose mother is a famous model.

Name_____ Date_____

COMMON CORE
STATE STANDARD
L.4.1a

Relative Adverbs

A **relative adverb** links two clauses together, and it gives more information about a word or phrase in the sentence. The relative adverbs are **where**, **when**, and **why**.

- That is the apartment building <u>where</u> my grandfather lives.
- The teacher gave us the reason <u>why</u> the experiment failed.
- She remembered a time <u>when</u> computers didn't exist.

Choose the correct relative adverb from the box that fits with each sentence. Write it on the line.

where	when	why

1. Susan told Pedro about the time _____ she visited the Liberty Bell in Philadelphia, Pennsylvania.

2. That is the room _____ the committee will make its decision.

3. They will go to the beach _____ the sun rises.

4. Please find a seat _____ you will be comfortable.

5. A fever was the reason _____ Samir could not go to school.

6. That is the house _____ we used to live.

COMMON CORE
STATE STANDARD
L.4.1a

Name_____ Date_____

Relative Adverbs

Read each sentence and write the relative adverb on the line that correctly replaces the underlined phrase.

1. _____ The United States is the country <u>in which</u> fifty states are located.

2. _____ Do you know the reason <u>for which</u> she never called?

3. _____ The date July 4, 1776, was the time <u>in which</u> the United States adopted the Declaration of Independence.

4. _____ One reason <u>for which</u> Alaska draws many visitors each year is the beauty of the state.

5. _____ The bridge is the point <u>at which</u> you take a left turn.

6. _____ This is the step in the recipe <u>in which</u> you should add the milk.

7. _____ Marta does not know the reason <u>for which</u> she was chosen.

8. _____ This is the wall <u>on which</u> we will place the framed picture.

9. _____ The pasture is the place <u>at which</u> you will find the cows grazing.

10. _____ That was the time <u>in which</u> the student was supposed to meet Mr. Wilton.

Name_____ Date_____

COMMON CORE
STATE STANDARD
L.4.1a

Relative Pronouns and Relative Adverbs

**Using a relative pronoun, combine the two sentences.
Write the new sentence on the lines.**

1. The vegetables are in the bag. The vegetables need to be put in the refrigerator.

   _____

   _____

2. This is the playground. I like to play at this playground in the summer.

   _____

   _____

3. He is a soccer player. He is also a kicker on the football team.

   _____

   _____

Read each sentence. Underline the relative adverb.

4. April was the month when Philip was born.

5. Not getting enough sunlight is the reason why the plant turned brown.

6. Autumn is the season when the leaves turn brilliant colors.

7. Paris is the place where the Eiffel Tower stands.

8. The restaurant where we ate dinner is right around the corner.

COMMON CORE
STATE STANDARD

L.4.1b

Progressive Tenses

COMMON CORE STATE STANDARD L.4.1b

Form and use the progressive (e.g., *I was walking; I am walking; I will be walking*) verb tenses.

Explain

Tell students that progressive verb forms tell about actions that are ongoing.

Say: *Verbs tell about actions, what's happening in a sentence or passage, or "to be" verbs. Sometimes these actions happened in the past or will take place in the future. Other times, the actions are ongoing. This means they are still happening or happen at the same time as something else. These are called progressive or continuous forms.*

Form the past progressive verb tense by using the "to be" verb *was* or *were* with an *-ing* verb.

Form the present progressive verb tense by using the "to be" verb *am*, *is*, or *are* with the *-ing* form of an action verb.

Form the future progressive verb tense by using the "to be" verb phrase *will be* with an *-ing* verb.

Model

Write this sentence on the board: *We are learning to play soccer as a team.*

Point out that the action of *learning to play as a team* is ongoing—the players learn to do it better with practice. The verb form is progressive because the lesson isn't learned once.

Guide Practice

Write the following verbs on the board: *was driving, is studying, will be attending.*

Ask a volunteer to use the first action, *was driving*, in a sentence as a past progressive. (Sample response: *My Aunt was driving when the snow began falling.*)

Ask: *Is the action ongoing? Or does it take place at the same time as another action? Is it past, present, or future progressive?*

Repeat the procedure with the remaining verbs. (Sample responses: *The scientist is studying fossils. Mom will be attending a workshop next week.*)

Name_____ Date_____

Past Progressive

Past progressive verb tense shows an action that took place in the past, over a period of time. Form the past progressive verb tense by using the "to be" verb **was** or **were** with an -**ing** verb.

- I <u>was singing</u> that song yesterday.
- We <u>were eating</u> dinner when the phone rang.

Rewrite each sentence below using the past progressive verb tense. Remember to use *was* or *were* and an *-ing* verb.

1. Sara jumps. _____

2. They walk. _____

3. He leaves. _____

Write a sentence using the past progressive verb tense of each verb in the box.

behave	chew	earn

4. _____

_____

5. _____

_____

6. _____

_____

COMMON CORE
STATE STANDARD
L.4.1b

Name_____ Date_____

Past Progressive

Complete the following sentences using past progressive forms of the verbs.

1. When Maria arrived in class, the teacher (collect)

   _____ homework assignments.

2. I (listen) _____ to music when I heard a knock at the door.

3. We (sing) _____ along with the radio.

4. Jen (pedal) _____ hard, but she could not catch up with her brother.

5. The firefighter (speak) _____ during a tour of the fire station.

6. Kim and Tanya (work) _____ on a science project all weekend.

7. Jim's dog (bark) _____ at people who were jogging past his yard.

8. The actors (rehearse) _____ the new play after school.

9. The students (study) _____ for the exam all week.

10. The sun (shine) _____ through my window this morning when I woke up.

Name_____ Date_____

COMMON CORE
STATE STANDARD
L.4.1b

Present Progressive

Present progressive verb tense tells about an ongoing action. The action is happening as it is said or written. Form the present progressive verb tense by using the "to be" verbs **am**, **is**, or **are** with the -**ing** form of an action verb.

- We <u>are going</u> to the store.
- She <u>is walking</u> the dog.
- I <u>am reading</u> my favorite book.

Complete the sentences using the correct present progressive form.

1. I (sleep) _____ on the sofa while Mom paints my room my favorite color.

2. Milly (watch) _____ the parade from the window.

3. Tomas and Jamal (play) _____ chess while they wait for their parents.

4. Uncle Morris (bake) _____ apples we picked at the orchard.

5. The ladybug (crawl) _____ along the flower stem.

6. Her sisters (paint) _____ posters for the spring concert at school.

COMMON CORE
STATE STANDARD
L.4.1b

Name_____ Date_____

Present Progressive

Choose six verbs from the list below. Use the verbs in a sentence using the present progressive form.

study	borrow	sniff	shrug	gasp	limp	blend
blink	crouch	deliver	yawn	spy	shut	drag

1. _____

_____

2. _____

_____

3. _____

_____

4. _____

_____

5. _____

_____

6. _____

_____

Name_____ Date_____

COMMON CORE
STATE STANDARD
L.4.1b

Future Progressive

> **Future progressive verb** tense tells about an action that will take place at a later time. Form the future progressive verb tense by using the "to be" verb **will be** with an **-ing** verb.
>
> - We <u>will be reading</u> a new book in class tomorrow.
> - Next week we <u>will be floating</u> down the river!

Complete each sentence using the future progressive form of the verb in parentheses.

1. Next week we (celebrate) _____ my best friend's birthday at the park.

2. Emma's dog (wiggle) _____ when he sees her bus coming.

3. If he hasn't finished his homework, Roger (stall)

_____ the teacher with a long story.

4. After we wash the dishes, we (mop) _____ the kitchen floor.

5. In time, the paint (fade) _____ from the sunlight hitting the wall.

6. When the runners reach the top of the hill, they (pause)

_____ to catch their breath.

COMMON CORE
STATE STANDARD
L.4.1b

Name_____ Date_____

Future Progressive

Choose six verbs from the list below. Use the verbs in a sentence using the future progressive form.

weave	treat	flood	forget	lift	trade
worry	arrange	decide	earn	sign	teach

1. _____

_____

2. _____

_____

3. _____

_____

4. _____

_____

5. _____

_____

6. _____

_____

Common Core Language Grade 4 • ©2014 Newmark Learning, LLC

Name_____ Date_____

Common Core
State Standard
L.4.1b

Progressive Tenses

Read the following passage. Write each underlined verb in the correct column of the chart.

My sister and I <u>are visiting</u> our grandmother this summer. Gram <u>has been making</u> dolls for many months. She <u>will be offering</u> them as prizes at a craft fair. The craft fair will help pay for my class trip. My sister and I <u>have been helping</u> by painting the dolls' faces. I <u>am sewing</u> pretty dresses for the dolls while my sister <u>is making</u> little wigs. By the time the craft fair begins, we <u>will have made</u> thirty dolls.

Past Progressive Tense	Present Progressive Tense	Future Progressive Tense

COMMON CORE
STATE STANDARD
L.4.1c

Modal Auxiliaries

> **COMMON CORE STATE STANDARD L.4.1c**
> Use modal auxiliaries (e.g., *can, may, must*) to convey various conditions.

Explain

Tell students that sometimes main verbs need helping verbs to express a meaning or idea.

Say: *The word* modal *is a grammar term that expresses a "mood" such as possibility, necessity, or time. The word* auxiliary *refers to something that helps or supports. So, a modal auxiliary is a verb that helps a main verb express a particular meaning or idea.*

Model

Write a list of modal auxiliaries on the board: *can, could, would, may, might, must, should,* and *will.* Then write the following sentence on the board: *Zack _____ walk his dog every day.* Try placing different modal auxiliaries in the sentence and point out how they affect the verb's meaning. *Must* he walk his dog? *Will* he walk his dog? *Should* he walk his dog?

Guide Practice

Write the following words on the board: *can, must, should.*

Ask a volunteer to write a sentence using the first word. (Sample response: *I can visit the zoo.*)

Ask: *How does the helping verb affect the meaning of the verb?* (Can expresses the ability to do something.) *What happens if we use a different helping verb in this sentence?*

Read the sentence aloud, substituting a different modal auxiliary verb. Point out the effect this has on the meaning of the verb.

Ask: *Why is it important to choose a modal auxiliary verb carefully?* (Because it helps express time or mood.)

Repeat the procedure with the remaining words. Have students write three sentences using these modal auxiliary verbs. Remind them that main verbs need helping verbs to express a meaning or idea.

COMMON CORE
STATE STANDARD
L.4.1c

Name_____ Date_____

Modal Auxiliaries

> **Modal auxiliary** verbs modify the main verb in a sentence. They help express possibility or necessity in a sentence, as well as mood or time.
>
> - I **can't** reach the box on the shelf.
> - You **could** try using a ladder.

Circle the correct modal auxiliary verb to complete each sentence.

1. When we get home, I (could, would) like a warm drink.

2. Lisa (must, may) apologize to her sister for breaking her bicycle.

3. Ramon and Sid (might, must) go swimming if it doesn't rain.

4. Rita promises she (will, could) play the guitar while Dan sings.

5. Mr. Lewis says we (should, could) read this book because we'll enjoy it.

6. Jenna (can't, must) enter her photo in the youth contest because she is twelve, and over the age limit.

7. The bus (may, would) arrive on time this morning.

8. I (will, would) like to go to the park tomorrow afternoon.

COMMON CORE
STATE STANDARD
L.4.1c

Name_____ Date_____

Modal Auxiliaries

Choose the modal auxiliary verb to correctly complete each sentence.

1. We (might, should) not be using Mom's computer without her permission.

2. Since Deanna has invited me, I (will, could) go to the movies with her this evening.

3. Kim (would, must) eat lunch before her father will let her play baseball with her friends.

4. Ricardo (may, should) borrow my book if he promises to take care of it.

5. Ms. Brown, (may, would) you like water or juice?

6. Building this experiment (could, must) take all weekend.

7. Laura (can, may) draw and paint very well.

8. If the weather is very warm, we (must, might) reschedule the hike for another day.

9. You really (must, could) see a doctor about that cut.

10. Paul (should, may) study for his test tonight if he wants to do well.

Common Core Language Grade 4 • ©2014 Newmark Learning, LLC

Name_____ Date_____

COMMON CORE
STATE STANDARD
L.4.1c

Modal Auxiliaries

Write a sentence using each modal auxiliary verb.

1. can

_____

2. could

_____

3. would

_____

4. may

_____

5. might

_____

6. must

_____

7. should

_____

8. will

_____

COMMON CORE
STATE STANDARD
L.4.1d

Order Adjectives

> **COMMON CORE STATE STANDARD L.4.1d**
> Order adjectives within sentences according to conventional patterns
> (e.g., *a small red bag* rather than *a red small bag*).

Explain

Tell students that adjectives in sentences should be placed in a special order so they can be more easily read and understood.

Say: *An adjective is a word that modifies and describes a noun. Some examples of common adjectives are* big, scary, colorful, *and* happy. *Sometimes writers use more than one adjective at a time. When this happens, writers usually put the adjectives in a special order. This helps make the sentences sound right and make sense.*

Model

Write these sentences on the board:

> *Three days ago, Carl bought a fast red sports car.*
> *Three days ago, Carl bought a red sports fast car.*

Underline the adjectives in these examples. Point out that the sentences have the same information, but the adjectives are in a different order. Point out that the order of adjectives is important for writing clear sentences. The adjectives *fast red sports* sound better than *red sports fast*. Sometimes the correct order of adjectives is easy to hear. Other times, it may require some thought. There are rules to help you choose the best order for your adjectives.

Guide Practice

Write these incomplete sentences on the board. Ask a volunteer to choose adjectives to complete them.

1. *On my aunt's birthday we took her to the _____ _____ restaurant.*
   (Example: *expensive Italian*)
2. *The _____ _____ train was so loud it made the floors of the house shake!* (Example: *long passenger*)
3. *Roberto rode his _____ _____ bike around the neighborhood so we could all see it.* (Example: *shiny new*)

Ask: *Did you write the adjectives in the correct order?*
Repeat the procedure with each sentence.

Tell the students to try reversing the order of these adjectives to see if that makes them sound better or worse. Remind them that adjectives should be placed in a special order so they can be more easily read and understood.

Name_____ Date_____

Order Adjectives

> **Adjectives** are words that modify and describe nouns.
> They should be ordered a certain way within sentences.
> The clearest order is usually:
>
> | **Opinion** | **Size** | **Feels/Looks** | **Age** |
> |---|---|---|---|
> | **Shape** | **Color** | **Nationality/Material** | **Purpose** |
>
> Incorrect:
>   My grandmother carries a <u>red</u> <u>small</u> bag.
> Correct:
>   My grandmother carries a <u>small</u> <u>red</u> bag.

**Choose adjectives from the box to complete the sentences.
Put the adjectives in the correct order within each sentence.**

tasty	metal	tiny	Canadian	colorful
shiny	friendly	plastic	old	red

1. When the _____ _____ dog started barking
   at us, we just laughed.

2. My _____ _____ pen-pal wrote me a letter
   over the weekend.

3. We like to visit the farmers' market for those _____
   _____ apples.

4. At John's birthday party, we put a _____
   _____ covering on the table.

5. I saw a _____ _____ suit of knight's armor
   at the museum yesterday.

COMMON CORE
STATE STANDARD
L.4.1d

Name_____ Date_____

Order Adjectives

Read these sentences. Then circle one sentence in each pair that uses adjectives in the correct order.

1. **a.** Our legs are sore because we ran in the difficult five-mile race.
    b. Our legs are sore because we ran in the five-mile difficult race.

2. **a.** Over the weekend I went to a hardware interesting store with Uncle Dave, and we bought paint.
    b. Over the weekend I went to an interesting hardware store with Uncle Dave, and we bought paint.

3. **a.** Maria could not sleep after she watched a horror scary movie alone on Friday night.
    b. Maria could not sleep after she watched a scary horror movie alone on Friday night.

4. **a.** Baseball is the oldest American sport that is still popular today.
    b. Baseball is the American oldest sport that is still popular today.

5. **a.** During his vacation, Arnold was excited to see the beautiful Mexican flag.
    b. During his vacation, Arnold was excited to see the Mexican beautiful flag.

Name_____ Date_____

Order Adjectives

Complete these sentences by adding at least two adjectives in the correct order on each blank.

1. Julio's friends enjoy watching _____ movies after school.

2. My family took a trip to the _____ museum over the weekend.

3. The _____ baseball player hit a home run to win the game.

4. There's no snack in the world as good as this

   _____ apple.

5. Matt was happy when he was done reading the

   _____ book.

6. The explorers found some _____ treasure in the hidden chest.

7. Uncle Terrence brought out our

   _____ coats on the cold morning.

8. We brought a bowl of food to the

   _____ dog in the yard.

9. Kiera giggled as she jumped into the

   _____ water and splashed around.

10. My new friend is a _____ student who shares many of my interests.

COMMON CORE
STATE STANDARD
L.4.1e

Form and Use Prepositional Phrases

> **COMMON CORE STATE STANDARD L.4.1e**
> Form and use prepositional phrases.

Explain

Prepositions introduce phrases that tell *where, when, what,* and *how.*

Say: *Prepositions are words we use to show relationships between words in a sentence. Prepositions introduce phrases that answer questions like where, when, what, and how.* Remind students of frequently occurring prepositions, such as *to, from, in, out, on, off, for, of, by, with, during, beyond,* and *toward.* Explain that these are only a few of the prepositions in the English language.

Model

Write the following sentence on the board: *We skated through the park across the street.*

Ask: *Where did we skate?* (through the park across the street) *Which words are prepositions that introduce the phrases?* (through, across)

Guide Practice

Write the following phrases:

1. *Choose a piece _____.*
2. *The train will arrive _____.*
3. *Gemma is walking _____.*
4. *The crowd applauded _____.*

Ask: *Do these sentences seem complete? Can we tell something more by adding prepositional phrases?* Write a question after each sentence: (1) *What?* (2) *When?* (3) *Where?* (4) *How?*

Ask a volunteer to complete the first sentence with a prepositional phrase, answering the question, *What?* (Sample response: *of fruit.*) Repeat the process with the remaining sentences. (Sample responses: *in the morning, across the street, with enthusiasm.*)

Have students complete the sentences in their notebooks, writing their own prepositional phrases. Have them underline the prepositional phrases. Remind them that prepositions tell *where, when, what,* and *how.*

Name_____ Date_____

COMMON CORE
STATE STANDARD
L.4.1e

Form and Use Prepositional Phrases

A preposition usually answers the questions <u>where</u>, <u>when</u>, <u>what</u>, and <u>how</u>. Prepositions usually introduce a **prepositional phrase**, which can consist of many parts.

- I dropped my hat **<u>onto</u>** <u>the dirty street</u>. (where)
- We usually nap **<u>in</u>** <u>the afternoon</u>. (when)

Read the passage. Underline the prepositional phrases.

Marta and June studied the book on Marta's desk. The photos of science projects seemed easy, but Marta was worried about the science fair. June began writing in her notebook. She made lists of things they had and things they needed. "I think it will be okay," she said with sympathy as she wrote. Marta's last building project for school had been a disaster. She remembered with embarrassment the way her volcano had fallen apart and landed on the floor. Instead of giving up, this time she would work with June to make a great project over the weekend.

Write a complete sentence using at least one prepositional phrase to answer each question.

1. Where do you like to go?

_____

_____

2. When do you have fun?

_____

_____

COMMON CORE
STATE STANDARD
L.4.1e

Name_____ Date_____

Form Prepositional Phrases

Choose six prepositions from the box.
Use each one in a sentence to form a prepositional phrase.

above	across	from	on	under	beyond
until	through	near	of	during	before

1. _____

_____

2. _____

_____

3. _____

_____

4. _____

_____

5. _____

_____

6. _____

_____

Name_____ Date_____

COMMON CORE
STATE STANDARD
L.4.1e

Use Prepositional Phrases

Complete each sentence with one or more prepositional phrases.

1. Katrina raced her brother _____

_____

2. Greg hid his sister's book _____

_____

3. Would you like lunch _____

_____

4. Tomas and Jamal shouted _____

_____

5. The yellow bird swooped _____

_____

6. Mom's friends visited _____

_____

7. My grandparents enjoyed _____

_____

8. The rain fell _____

_____

COMMON CORE
STATE STANDARD
L.4.1f

Produce Complete Sentences

> **COMMON CORE STATE STANDARD L.4.1f**
> Produce complete sentences, recognizing and correcting inappropriate fragments and run-ons.

Explain
Every complete sentence contains a subject, verb, and complete thought.

Say: *A sentence should contain a subject, verb, and complete thought. We know how to use simple, compound, and complex sentences. Sometimes when we revise and edit, we find incomplete sentences that we need to correct.*

Model
Write the following on the board:

> *When we travel by bus. We like to look out of the windows at the scenery it makes the time pass quickly.*

Say: *As writers, we need to use complete sentences. Reread your text to check for sentence fragments and run-ons. Demonstrate different ways to correct the sentence fragment and run-on sentence.* (Sample response: When we travel by bus, we like to look out of the windows at the scenery; it makes the time pass quickly.)

Guide Practice
Write the following sentences on the board:

> *Ginger barked and ran down the hill she was chasing a squirrel. That climbed the fence.*

Ask a volunteer to correct the run-on sentence. (Sample response: *Ginger barked and ran down the hill. She was chasing a squirrel that climbed the fence.*)

Ask: *Is there another way to correct this? Could we write it as one sentence using different punctuation?* (Sample response: *Ginger barked and ran down the hill; she was chasing a squirrel that climbed the fence.*)

Have students write the sentence in their notebooks, showing several ways to correct the run-on and sentence fragment. Remind them that every sentence should contain a complete thought.

COMMON CORE
STATE STANDARD
L.4.1f

Name_____ Date_____

Produce Complete Sentences

Every **complete sentence** contains a subject and a predicate.
A sentence is a complete thought.

Complete

I put the frog in my backpack.

The thunder scared us all.

Incomplete

Took it home to show my brother.

At least six inches of rain.

Circle the complete sentences.

1. What time will they be here?

2. A high-speed boat.

3. The short story about a man with a creepy garden.

4. She ate lunch with her mother and brother.

5. Anytime they want to talk.

6. Traveled back in time and was transported to present-day Europe.

7. They climbed over the mountain and crossed the bridge.

8. Karen had a strange dream about horses and presidents, which caused her to wake up late for work.

9. The breeze flowed through the flowers in the garden, causing petals to drop onto the grass.

10. That polinate the flowers and produce honey that we can buy at the store and eat.

COMMON CORE
STATE STANDARD
L.4.1f

Name_____ Date_____

Produce Complete Sentences

Complete the following sentences.

1. Marcia and Ellen _____

_____

2. After the movie, we _____

_____

3. _____

before we found the book.

4. My neighbor's dog _____

_____

5. When we opened the door _____

_____

6. As the wind began to blow_____

_____

7. The lightning_____

_____

8. _____

until we arrived at the movie theater.

Name_____ Date_____

Produce Complete Sentences: Recognize Fragments

Read each fragment. Combine them to form complete sentences.

1. The smallest kitten in the box. Made the most noise.

_____

_____

2. It was very dark. Marcus and Gerry were sure they heard a noise. Coming from the next room.

_____

_____

3. When the wind picked up. The leaves scattered across the yard and caught in the fence.

_____

_____

4. The girls followed the rabbit. They saw in the park. To see where it was going.

_____

_____

5. A ball of yarn rolled across the floor. After I knocked over the basket.

_____

_____

6. Mother enjoys seeing the daffodils blooming. In her garden in April.

_____

_____

COMMON CORE
STATE STANDARD

L.4.1f

Name_____ Date_____

Produce Complete Sentences: Recognize Run-Ons

Read each group of words. Rewrite them to form complete sentences.

1. Molly had to change her shoes they were wet from the rain.

_____

_____

2. Dad writes everything on his calendar he hates to forget about basketball games.

_____

_____

3. Would you like some hot soup it will warm you up.

_____

_____

4. Tomas carried his skateboard up the hill it was too steep to ride.

_____

_____

5. The baby laughed when she saw the butterfly she cried when it flew away.

_____

_____

6. It was raining hard Ms. Walker closed her fruit stand and went home.

_____

_____

Name_____ Date_____

COMMON CORE
STATE STANDARD
L.4.1f

Produce Complete Sentences: Fragments and Run-Ons

Read the following passage. Rewrite it in the space below, using complete sentences.

Ladybug beetles are very useful. In the garden. They eat insects such as aphids, which eat plants, ladybugs protect our plants by eating these pests. Ladybugs don't have to worry too much about being eaten. When they're at work in the garden. Their red wings warn birds to stay away ladybugs taste terrible. Ladybugs have another defense, too. They can release liquid. That tastes bad from their legs.

_____

_____

_____

_____

_____

_____

_____

_____

COMMON CORE
STATE STANDARD
L.4.1g

Correctly Use Frequently Confused Words

COMMON CORE STATE STANDARD L.4.1g
Correctly use frequently confused words (e.g., *to, too, two; there, their*).

Explain
Tell students sometimes words sound alike but mean different things. It's important they learn the difference between words that are often confused.

Say: *Sometimes we are confused by words that sound alike. We must remember how to spell and use words that sound similar, such as* t-h-e-i-r *and* t-h-e-r-e, *so we use them correctly.*

Model
Write the words *hear* and *here* on the board, along with the following sentences: *I _____ the music playing. I will listen to the music _____.*

Say: *Though the words sound the same, they look very different and have different meanings.*

Guide Practice
Write the following words on the board: *to, too, two.*

Ask a volunteer to write a sentence using the first word.

Ask: *What does this word mean?* (toward) *How should it be used?* (as an adverb or preposition) Repeat the procedure with the remaining words.

Say: *We see how easy it could be to confuse words that sound the same:* to, *meaning in the direction of;* too, *meaning also, and* two, *meaning the number between one and three.*

Have students write a sentence using each of the three words. Remind them to check the spelling of each word to make sure they are using it correctly.

Name_____ Date_____

COMMON CORE STATE STANDARD
L.4.1g

Correctly Use Frequently Confused Words

There are many words that sound alike but mean different things. They can be easily confused unless we remember them.

- **made**: to form something by putting parts together
  I <u>made</u> my lunch before school.
- **maid**: a female who does cleaning work
  The <u>maid</u> came to our hotel room to clean.

Write a sentence using each word. Check the meanings of the words to be sure you are using them correctly.

1. dear _____

   _____

2. deer _____

   _____

3. hair _____

   _____

4. hare _____

   _____

5. it's _____

   _____

6. its _____

   _____

COMMON CORE
STATE STANDARD

L.4.1g

Name_____ Date_____

Correctly Use Frequently Confused Words

Circle the correct word to complete each sentence.

1. Marlow asked if (eye, I) wanted to go to his house after school.

2. Jake watched the (be, bee) land on the daisy.

3. Susan couldn't (hear, here) the speaker because the class was so loud.

4. After baseball practice, (their, there, they're) going to the playground.

5. Mike had a (plain, plane) bagel after school.

6. They (we're, were) laughing at all of his jokes.

7. Remember to (close, clothes) the door when you leave.

8. The ranchers rounded up the (heard, herd) of cattle.

Write a sentence using each word correctly.

9. right _____

   _____

   _____

10. write _____

   _____

   _____

Common Core Language Grade 4 • ©2014 Newmark Learning, LLC

Name_____ Date_____

COMMON CORE
STATE STANDARD
L.4.1g

Correctly Use Frequently Confused Words

Circle eight words from the box. Use each word in a sentence correctly.

you're	do	won	cord	dessert	see	eight	no	knew
your	due	one	cored	desert	sea	ate	know	new

1. _____

_____

2. _____

_____

3. _____

_____

4. _____

_____

5. _____

_____

6. _____

_____

7. _____

_____

8. _____

_____

COMMON CORE
STATE STANDARD

L.4.2a

Use Correct Capitalization

> **COMMON CORE STATE STANDARD L.4.2a**
> Use correct capitalization.

Explain
Tell students that proper nouns in sentences should be capitalized.

Say: *A proper noun names a specific person, place, or thing and begins with a capital letter no matter where it appears in a sentence. Words that are capitalized include days, months, holidays, product names, specific places, languages, nationalities, and important words in titles.*

Model
Write these sentences on the board:

> *During her class trip, Angela went to the Washington Monument.*
> *My favorite book is* Through the Looking-Glass *by Lewis Carroll.*
> *My grandmother likes to shop at Macy's.*

Underline the proper nouns in the examples. Point out that *Angela* and *Washington Monument* are proper nouns and should be capitalized because they are the names of a particular person and a particular place. Point out that *Through the Looking-Glass* is a title and *Lewis Carroll* is a person and both should be capitalized. Point out that *Macy's* is the name of a department store.

Guide Practice
Write these sentences on the board. Ask a volunteer to underline the proper nouns in the first sentence.

1. *Mr. whit's students did not have class on labor day.* (<u>whit's</u>, <u>labor day</u>)
2. *Jin toured penn state university with his older sister jill.* (<u>Jin</u>, <u>penn state university</u>, <u>jill</u>)
3. *My mom learned to speak french at a school in paris, france.*) <u>french</u>, <u>paris</u>, <u>france</u>)

Have the students find the proper nouns in the remaining sentences. Remind them that a proper noun is the specific name of a person, place, or thing.

Common Core Language Grade 4 • ©2014 Newmark Learning, LLC

Name_____ Date_____

Use Correct Capitalization

> A **proper noun** names a specific person, place, or thing.
> A proper noun is always capitalized no matter where it
> appears in a sentence.
>
> - My sister **A**lma's favorite juice is **J**ammin' **C**ooler.
> - The teacher asked us to read ***N**ate the **G**reat* by
>   **M**arjorie **W**einman **S**harmat.
> - He went to see the film ***D**iary of a **W**impy **K**id*.
>
> **Underline the proper nouns in the following sentences.**

1. My boy scouts leader is from mexico.

2. The class planted trees on arbor day with their teacher mrs. gibbons.

3. My favorite restaurant is slice of pizza pizzeria located on falls boulevard.

4. My brother ernesto wants to attend berkeley college and major in english.

5. My family visits roba's farm in october to pick apples and pumpkins.

6. This year I am dressing up as batman for halloween.

7. She speaks french and spanish.

8. One of my favorite movies is nightmare before christmas.

9. The capital of russia is moscow.

10. We are going on a cruise from italy to spain, and we will sail across the

mediterranean sea.

COMMON CORE
STATE STANDARD
L.4.2a

Name_____ Date_____

Use Correct Capitalization

Rewrite these sentences using the correct capitalization of the proper nouns.

1. Randy and rex live on 231 thompson street in the town of hillshire.

_____

_____

2. My favorite book is *freckle juice,* by judy blume.

_____

_____

3. My sister marilyn attends the university of
pennsylvania, where she studies spanish and french.

_____

_____

4. On tuesday, may 5, 2005, I visited the
empire state building in new york city.

_____

_____

5. Reggie buys used books at a store called almost new,
which is located on main street near peggy sue's deli.

_____

_____

COMMON CORE
STATE STANDARD
L.4.2a

Name_____ Date_____

Use Correct Capitalization

Write a proper noun for each common noun on the blank line provided.

1. street name _____

2. ocean _____

3. boy's name _____

4. city _____

5. girl's name _____

6. country _____

7. state _____

8. movie title _____

9. holiday _____

10. planet _____

COMMON CORE
STATE STANDARD
L.4.2b

Use Commas and Quotation Marks

> **COMMON CORE STATE STANDARD L.4.2b**
> Use commas and quotation marks to mark direct speech and quotations from a text.

Explain

Tell students we use commas and quotation marks to mark direct speech and quotations.

Say: *Direct speech is the words a character says in a story. A quotation is the words a real or fictional person says as quoted, or repeated, by another speaker or writer. In writing, quotation marks show the exact words the character or person speaks.*

Model

Write the following sentences on the board:

President Roosevelt said, "The only thing we have to fear is fear itself."
"The only thing we have to fear is fear itself," said President Roosevelt.
President Roosevelt said fear was holding our nation back.

Point out the placement of commas and quotation marks in the first and second sentences. Point out the third sentence, which does not include a quotation.

Guide Practice

Display the following sentences on the board. Ask a volunteer to decide if the first sentence contains a quotation or direct speech. If so, have the student add punctuation and make any other changes.

A thing of beauty is a joy forever said John Keats.
Dad said we'll have to stay in the backyard today.
Dad said Please rake the leaves and put them in this bag.

Ask: *Does the first sentence contain a quotation or direct speech? Were you able to correctly add the punctuation?*
Repeat the procedure with the remaining sentences.

Have the students copy the sentences in their notebooks, making changes to indicate any quotations. Remind them that writers tell the names of speakers outside the quotation marks and that the punctuation the writer uses depends on where the speaker's name appears.

Name_____ Date_____

COMMON CORE
STATE STANDARD
L.4.2b

Use Commas and Quotation Marks for Direct Speech

> **Commas** and **quotation marks** show direct speech.
> Quotation marks surround the speaker's words.
>
> - If the quote comes <u>before</u> the person who spoke, place a comma after the quote, but within the quotation marks.
>
>   "Please turn to page five," said the teacher.
>
> - If the quote comes <u>after</u> the person who spoke, place a comma before the quotes.
>
>   She yelled, "Dinner is ready!"

Rewrite each item to show the direct speech.

1. Oh, I can carry it the child said cheerfully. It isn't heavy.

_____

2. Mine is a long and a sad tale! said Mouse, turning to Alice.

_____

3. Which direction should I go? she asked.

_____

4. I don't see said Caterpillar.

_____

5. By the powers, Ben Gunn! roared Silver.

_____

COMMON CORE
STATE STANDARD
L.4.2b

Name_____ Date_____

Use Commas and Quotation Marks for Direct Speech

Rewrite each item with correct punctuation.

1. When will he come home, Marmee? asked Beth, with a little quiver.

_____

_____

2. Alice crawled into the chair, sighing This has been quite a day.

_____

_____

3. Goodness, just look at the time! cried Nancy as she rose to her feet.

_____

_____

4. Hannah, please pour a glass of water for Mrs. Ritter, suggested Carla.

_____

_____

5. Don't mind me. I'm as happy as a cricket here, answered Jo.

_____

_____

Name_____ Date_____

COMMON CORE
STATE STANDARD
L.4.2b

Use Commas and Quotation Marks for Direct Speech

Rewrite the sentences as direct speech using commas and quotation marks.

1. Rachel said she will buy milk after she returns her library books.

_____

_____

2. Tomas asked what time practice will start.

_____

_____

3. Liz shouted to the bus driver to stop and wait for her.

_____

_____

4. Kim said she saw a sea lion when she visited the aquarium Saturday.

_____

_____

5. Mom insisted that I wear a hat this morning because it was cold out.

_____

_____

COMMON CORE
STATE STANDARD
L.4.2b

Name_____ Date_____

Use Commas and Quotation Marks for Quotations

Directly quoting a speaker is similar to direct speech.

- If the quote comes <u>before</u> the speaker is cited, the comma goes before the last quotation mark.

    "Whatever you are, be a good one," said Abraham Lincoln.

- If the quote comes <u>after</u> the speaker is cited, the comma goes before the quotation marks.

    Benjamin Franklin once said, "Honesty is the best policy."

Read each sentence. Rewrite each one to show the quotations.

1. Aristotle once said a friend to all is a friend to none.

_____

_____

2. The only way to have a friend is to be one said Ralph Waldo Emerson.

_____

_____

3. Try not to become a man of success, said Albert Einstein, but rather try to become a man of value.

_____

_____

4. According to Woody Allen eighty percent of success is showing up.

_____

_____

Name_____ Date_____

COMMON CORE
STATE STANDARD
L.4.2b

Use Commas and Quotation Marks for Quotations

Read each sentence. Rewrite each one to show the quotations.

1. Honesty is the first chapter in the book of wisdom said President Thomas Jefferson.

_____

_____

2. According to the poet Robert Frost a poem begins in delight and ends in wisdom.

_____

_____

3. President John F. Kennedy once said that a child miseducated is a child lost.

_____

_____

4. All that I am, or hope to be, said President Abraham Lincoln, I owe to my angel mother.

_____

_____

5. Playwright William Shakespeare wrote the course of true love never did run smooth.

_____

_____

COMMON CORE
STATE STANDARD
L.4.2b

Name_____ Date_____

Use Commas and Quotation Marks for Quotations

Read each sentence. Rewrite each one to show the quotations.

1. The time to repair the roof is when the sun is shining said President John F. Kennedy.

   _____

   _____

2. According to Confucius life is really simple, but we insist on making it complicated.

   _____

   _____

3. William Shakespeare wrote love all, trust a few, do wrong to none.

   _____

   _____

4. Alone we can do so little; together we can do so much stated Helen Keller.

   _____

   _____

5. I know that I am intelligent said Socrates because I know that I know nothing.

   _____

   _____

Name_____ Date_____

COMMON CORE
STATE STANDARD
L.4.2b

Use Commas and Quotation Marks for Direct Speech and Quotations

Read the following passage. Rewrite it using commas and quotation marks to show direct speech and quotations.

Ms. Martinez sat down next to her daughter, Rosie, on the bench.

What's the score? she asked, looking across the field.

Three to five, Rosie answered. Rosie played soccer, too. She wanted

to get better, so she watched a lot of good teams play. She hoped to

learn some of their skills.

Rosie blinked. I heard someone talking about something

Yogi Berra said, and I decided he had the right idea.

What did Yogi Berra say? her mother asked.

You can observe a lot by watching. Rosie grinned.

_____

_____

_____

_____

_____

_____

_____

Use a Comma in a Compound Sentence

COMMON CORE
STATE STANDARD
L.4.2c

COMMON CORE STATE STANDARD L.4.2c
Use a comma before a coordinating conjunction in a compound sentence.

Explain
Tell students that we use a comma before a coordinating conjunction when forming compound sentences.

Say: *Coordinating conjunctions are words such as* and, but, for, nor, yet, *and* or. *Use coordinating conjunctions to combine two sentences into compound sentences. Use a comma before the coordinating conjunction.*

Model
Display this text for students:

Emma bought a green shirt. She borrowed her sister's shorts. Emma already had shorts. She wanted something new to wear on a field trip.

Say: *These sentences sound a little boring. Using all short, simple sentences makes the writing choppy. Listen to the difference when the writer combines some of these sentences into compound sentences with a comma and coordinating conjunction.*

Make the following changes to the passage:

Emma bought a green shirt, and she borrowed her sister's shorts. Emma already had shorts, but she wanted something new to wear on a field trip.

Point out the coordinating conjunctions used to create compound sentences. Show students how the coordinating conjunctions work by showing the relationships between ideas. Point out the commas before the coordinating conjunctions.

Guide Practice
Write these sentence pairs on the board:

Manny answered the telephone. It was ringing.
The cat tried to sleep. Her kittens jumped on her.
Gwen enjoys painting. She didn't enter the art contest.

Ask a volunteer to write a compound sentence using the first pair of sentences. (*Manny answered the telephone, for it was ringing.*)

Point out the use of the comma before the coordinating conjunction. Repeat the procedure with the remaining sentence pairs.

Name_____ Date_____

COMMON CORE
STATE STANDARD
L.4.2c

Use a Comma Before a Coordinating Conjunction in a Compound Sentence

Combine two simple sentences to make a compound sentence. Connect simple sentences by using a **comma** and a **coordinating conjunction**.

Coordinating Conjunctions: *for, nor, yet, but, and, or, so*

We are eating dinner, **and** then we are seeing a movie.

Roger didn't like country music, **nor** did he like jazz.

Read the following pairs of sentences. Combine each pair to form a compound sentence.

1. Kim is bringing a tent. Roger will help to set it up.

_____

2. It didn't rain yesterday. It didn't rain last night.

_____

3. Tammy may read a magazine. She may read a book.

_____

4. The roses are beautiful. My sister prefers daisies.

_____

5. The sun is shining. We feel very cold.

_____

COMMON CORE
STATE STANDARD
L.4.2c

Name_____ Date_____

Use a Comma Before a Coordinating Conjunction in a Compound Sentence

Read the following passage. Rewrite it using coordinating conjunctions to create compound sentences.

Jenna and Ricardo both have brothers. Their brothers are very different. Jenna's brother, Paul, likes to run. He joined the school track team. Paul wins a lot of races. He's very humble. Ricardo's brother, Tomas, likes to cook. He makes dinner for his family on Sundays. Tomas can make vegetable soup. He can make pancakes. Jenna and Ricardo could learn from their brothers. They have never asked Paul and Tomas to teach them new skills.

_____

_____

_____

_____

_____

_____

_____

_____

_____

_____

Common Core Language Grade 4 • ©2014 Newmark Learning, LLC

Name_____ Date_____

COMMON CORE
STATE STANDARD
L.4.2c

Use a Comma Before a Coordinating Conjunction in a Compound Sentence

Read the following pairs of sentences. Combine each pair to form a compound sentence.

1. My sister likes yogurt. She's allergic to dairy foods.

_____

_____

2. We were out of bananas. We went to the market.

_____

_____

3. Miguel has a new skateboard. He prefers to ride the old one.

_____

_____

4. You may do your homework at your desk. You may take it to the library.

_____

_____

5. Vic won't eat tomatoes. He won't eat squash.

_____

_____

6. Mom is painting the living room. The wallpaper is old and faded.

_____

_____

COMMON CORE
STATE STANDARD
L.4.2d

Using Reference Materials to Spell

> **COMMON CORE STATE STANDARD L.4.2d**
> Spell grade-appropriate words correctly, consulting references as needed.

Explain

Tell students that some words can be difficult to spell. Students can use reference materials to check and correct their spelling.

Say: *Writers use reference materials to help find the correct spelling of a word they do not know. Reference materials may be glossaries (word lists), dictionaries, computer spell-checkers, or other materials. There are many ways to check and correct spelling.*

Model

Write the following words on the board:

> flour [flowr] n. finely ground grain used for baking
> flower [flow-er] n. a blossom that blooms on a plant; v. to produce flowers

Say: *These are example words in a dictionary. The words in a dictionary are in alphabetical order. Guide words, the first and last words on a page, are listed on the tops of pages. These can help you find the words you are looking for. The terms in brackets ([ ]) show you how to say the word. The n. means "noun." The v. means "verb." There are other parts of speech, too.*

Look at the words *flour* and *flower*. They look and sound alike, but they are very different. Ask students which word they would look up if they were writing about making a cake (*flour*). Then, ask which they would look up if they were writing about a garden (*flower*). A few letters make a big difference! That is one reason why correct spelling is very important.

Guide Practice

Provide students with a dictionary and ask them to look up the meanings of the following words: *tangle, hinge, ordinary*

Remind students that guide words on the tops of pages help them know which words are found on each page. Each dictionary entry includes a word's correct spelling, pronunciation, parts of speech, and definition.

Name_____ Date_____

COMMON CORE
STATE STANDARD
L.4.2d

Spell Grade-Appropriate Words Correctly Using Reference Materials

Reference materials such as dictionaries, glossaries, and spell-checkers can help you learn to spell words correctly. When you aren't sure how to spell a word, turn to one of these guides for help.

Use these sample dictionary entries to find spelling errors in this paragraph. Underline the misspelled words and then write the correct spellings below the paragraph.

> **amazing** [a-mayz-ing] adj. wonderful or surprising
>
> **creature** [kree-chur] n. a living thing; an animal
>
> **curious** [kyoor-e-us] adj. wanting to learn more
>
> **elephant** [el-e-fant] n. a large, heavy animal with a trunk
>
> **favorite** [fa-ver-ite] adj. liked more than other things
>
> **frightening** [frite-en-ing] adj. causing fear
>
> **giraffes** [je-rafs] n. tall four-legged animals with long necks

My family visited the zoo last weekend to see the animals. I'd learned about giraffes at school and was curios about how they really looked. They were amazing! I've never seen an animal that was so tall before. My brother liked seeing the lions, but they were a little too fritening for me. My favorite animal was the elafant. What a large creeture it was! It looked bigger than Mom's van. We had a very interesting day at the zoo, and I'm eager to go back.

_____

_____

COMMON CORE
STATE STANDARD
L.4.2d

Name_____ Date_____

Spell Grade-Appropriate Words Correctly Using Reference Materials

Read the sentences. Then find the misspelled word in each sentence. Using the dictionary excerpt below, write the correct spelling of the word on the line.

spectacle [SPEK-tih-kul] *n.* 1. an uncommon or impressive show, such as fireworks. 2. a pair of eyeglasses

spectacular [SPEK-TA-kyuh-ler] *adj.* beautiful or dramatic; impressive

spectator [SPEK-tay-ter] *n.* someone who watches an event, such as a show or game, but does not take part in it

spectrum [SPEK-trum] *n.* the band of colors seen in a rainbow

speculate [SPEH-kyuh-late] *v.* to guess, think deeply, or ponder

1. My family watches the spektaculur fireworks show on the river during the fourth of July every year.

   _____

2. We love going to the circus because it is such a huge spectucel.

   _____

3. When she refused to tell them where she was going, they had to spekulat the answer.

   _____

4. Paul, a former professional soccer player, now enjoys being a spektater at the games.

   _____

COMMON CORE
STATE STANDARD
L.4.2d

Name_____ Date_____

Spell Grade-Appropriate Words
Correctly Using Reference Materials

Choose two words from the word box, and look up each word in a dictionary. Then fill in the information boxes for each word.

irrigation	triumph	souvenir	helicopter
stubborn	manufacture	independence	melody

Word #1

Word spelling: _____

Guide words on dictionary page:

_____

One definition of this word:

_____

Write a sentence using this word:

_____

Word #2

Word spelling: _____

Guide words on dictionary page:

_____

One definition of this word:

_____

Write a sentence using this word:

_____

COMMON CORE
STATE STANDARD
L.4.3a

Choose Words and Phrases to Convey Ideas Precisely

> **COMMON CORE STATE STANDARD L.4.3a**
> Choose words and phrases to convey ideas precisely.

Explain
Tell students that when they write, they must choose the right word to describe a person, place, thing, or scene precisely.

Say: *When you choose words or phrases to convey ideas precisely, readers or listeners clearly understand what you want to say.*

Model
On the board, write two sentences:

> *Two children got on the bus.*
> *The small boy elbowed past his sister, scampered down the narrow aisle of the school bus, and slid across the cracked seat to sit by the window.*

Point out that in the first example, different people hearing this sentence could picture the scene many different ways. But the description in the second sentence is more exact. Any listener would picture the scene in about the same way.

Guide Practice
On the board, write four headings—*Adjectives, Adverbs, Nouns,* and *Verbs*. Under the appropriate heading, write the following descriptive words: *sour, hungrily, minivan,* and *flutter*.

Ask a volunteer to add a word to one of the lists. Then ask more students to add to the lists.

Ask: *How do these words help express your ideas?*

Have the students write sentences using descriptive words. Remind them that nouns and verbs can also be descriptive.

Common Core Language Grade 4 • ©2014 Newmark Learning, LLC

Name_____ Date_____

COMMON CORE
STATE STANDARD
L.4.3a

Choose Words and Phrases to Convey Ideas Precisely

It is important to choose words carefully when speaking or writing in order to **convey ideas precisely**. The right words give the reader or listener a clear picture. Compare these two sentences:

- The boy swam.
- He methodically swam laps up and down the lanes of the Olympic-sized pool.

Underline the descriptive words in the following story.

I was astonished when my Uncle Jake said I had to invent an original frozen yogurt flavor for his awesome shop, Tenth Avenue Yogurt Factory. He wanted something extreme that kids in my school would gobble up and then come back for more. He already had some crazy flavors, like sweet potato cashew and french fry and ketchup. My mission was to take yogurt to infinity and beyond. I jumped into the project with a list of foods I see kids eating at lunch time. The first two on the list were peanut butter and mac and cheese. I also recalled that my best friend Eli puts peanut butter on his grilled cheese sandwiches and insists that it's delicious. I spent four days making lists and thinking and talking to my classmates. Then I told Uncle Jake what the brand-new flavor must be: peanut butter with mac and cheese.

COMMON CORE
STATE STANDARD
L.4.3a

Name_____ Date_____

Choose Words and Phrases to Convey Ideas Precisely

Use adjectives to make these sentences more descriptive.
Use more than one adjective for a noun if needed.

1. Christine's _____ horse won both

   _____ races at the _____ rodeo.

2. Matt's _____ cake was quickly eaten up at the

   _____ celebration at the _____ courthouse.

3. The _____ bus climbed the _____

   hill on a _____ afternoon.

4. My _____ cousin Gino goes hiking on

   the _____ trails that weave up the

   _____ hills behind his house.

5. Becky likes _____ pizza, especially the kind from

   the _____ shop over in the _____ mall.

Add an adverb to each sentence to make it more descriptive.

6. Bella _____ does her homework during class.

7. After the teacher finished explaining the assignment, Tommy
   _____ started working on his essay.

8. Tristan went to the front of the room and _____
   waited for his turn to play.

9. At the zoo, we saw two cheetahs _____ running
   after a toy.

10. Katie _____ shared her raisin bun with her sister.

Common Core Language Grade 4 • ©2014 Newmark Learning, LLC

Name_____ Date_____

COMMON CORE
STATE STANDARD
L.4.3a

Choose Words and Phrases to Convey Ideas Precisely

The sentences below need to be rewritten so the writer conveys ideas more clearly. Using precise words and phrases, rewrite the sentences so they form pictures in the reader's mind.

1. Someone went downtown.

_____

_____

2. A man played an instrument.

_____

_____

3. He was tired.

_____

_____

4. A woman sat down.

_____

_____

5. They bought shoes.

_____

_____

6. She got a pet.

_____

_____

COMMON CORE
STATE STANDARD
L.4.3b

Choose Punctuation for Effect

> **COMMON CORE STATE STANDARD L.4.3b**
> Choose punctuation for effect.

Explain

Review how punctuation in writing is like road signs in driving. Punctuation marks say "stop" or "slow down." They show when someone is saying something. They help the reader understand what the writer means.

Say: *Punctuation can give more information to the reader. It can add emotion or tone to a piece of writing.*

Parentheses add information but are not necessary to the meaning of the sentence. Punctuation goes inside the parentheses if it belongs to the information within; it goes outside the parentheses if it's part of the sentence

Quotation marks show when a person is speaking.

A dash adds emphasis. It is a stronger stop than a comma, but doesn't separate like parentheses.

An exclamation mark adds emotion to a sentence. Used with an interjection, like "oh, no!" it shows that strong emotion is intended.

Model

Write the following sentences on the board:

1. *Dad said, "Don't be late for dinner."*
2. *We left the park at 5:30—we checked Sarah's watch.*
3. *Sarah's watch was wrong, so we were late. Dad was mad!*

Discuss each example. Point out how each type of punctuation affects how the sentence is read.

Guide Practice

Write these sentences on the board. Ask a volunteer to add punctuation for effect to each sentence.

1. *Oh gosh I forgot to buy dog food* (exclamation mark or marks)
2. *I was sorry when Ms. Green left she was my favorite teacher.* (dash)
3. *Oh no said Patti I lost my library book.* (exclamation mark, period, and quotation marks)
4. *I asked actually I begged my parents to let me get a puppy.* (parentheses)

Name_____ Date_____

COMMON CORE
STATE STANDARD
L.4.3b

Choose Punctuation for Effect

Punctuation guides the reader and helps them understand the meaning of sentences. Writers can use punctuation to add emotion or create a certain tone.

- The only thing she could do—if she could do anything at all—was wait for her test scores to arrive.
- You could use sour cream (or greek yogurt) in the recipe.

Write a sentence including the type of punctuation listed.

1. dash

_____

_____

2. parentheses

_____

_____

3. quotation marks

_____

_____

4. exclamation mark

_____

_____

COMMON CORE
STATE STANDARD
L.4.3b

Name_____ Date_____

Choose Punctuation for Effect

Read each sentence. Then circle the sentence that is correctly punctuated.

1. **We're having spaghetti for dinner we always have spaghetti on Wednesday**

   a. (We're having spaghetti for dinner) we always have spaghetti on Wednesday
   b. We're having spaghetti for dinner, "we always have spaghetti on Wednesday."
   c. We're having spaghetti for dinner—we always have spaghetti on Wednesday.

2. **I'm really angry that you lost my scarf said JoAnn**

   a. "I'm really angry that you lost my scarf!" said JoAnn.
   b. I'm really angry that you lost my scarf, "said JoAnn"
   c. "I'm really angry that you lost my scarf" said JoAnn!

3. **My grandfather my father's father worked on the railroad**

   a. My grandfather "my father's father" worked on the railroad.
   b. My grandfather (my father's father) worked on the railroad.
   c. My grandfather my father's father worked on the railroad!

4. **No there is no such thing as a dragon**

   a. No, there is no such thing as a dragon.
   b. No there is no such thing as a dragon!
   c. No (there is no such thing as a dragon).

5. **We had a lot of fun at the carnival there was a roller coaster**

   a. We had a lot of fun at the carnival, there was a roller coaster.
   b. We had a lot of fun at the carnival! (there was a roller coaster)
   c. We had a lot of fun at the carnival—there was a roller coaster!

Name_____ Date_____

COMMON CORE
STATE STANDARD
L.4.3b

Choose Punctuation for Effect

Add parentheses to each sentence to make its meaning clear.

1. I told Juan at least I thought I did that the party is tonight.

2. We caught three kinds of fish trout, bluegills, and bass at the lake on Saturday.

Rewrite each sentence, adding dashes to make its meaning clear.

3. Did you get a letter the one from the school today?

_____

_____

4. Jack is kind, funny, and dependable he is my best friend.

_____

_____

Rewrite each sentence below, adding quotation marks and other punctuation to make the sentence clear.

5. The contest winners said Keesha are Winston and Nelson.

_____

_____

6. Don't you dare touch my teddy bear yelled my little sister.

_____

_____

COMMON CORE
STATE STANDARD
L.4.3c

Formal and Informal English

> **COMMON CORE STATE STANDARD L.4.3c**
> Differentiate between contexts that call for formal English (e.g., *presenting ideas*) and situations where informal discourse is appropriate (e.g., *small-group discussion*).

Explain
Tell students that we talk and write in different ways for different audiences.

Say: *We talk and write in different ways for different situations. For example, a student who is giving a presentation usually has more well-thought-out ideas and uses more complete sentences and a broader vocabulary than a student who is in a small-group discussion. A student who is writing a letter to a friend usually uses different language than he or she would use in speaking to the school principal.*

Informal	Formal
Tone is casual.	Tone is serious.
Some incomplete sentences.	Sentences are complete. Grammar is correct.
May use a lot of contractions and some slang.	Fewer contractions and little or no slang.

Model
Write these sentences on the board:

1. *Mrs. Stevens, may I please be excused?*

2. *Mrs. Stevens, can I go?*

Ask: *Which sentence is an example of formal English?* (first) *Which is an example of informal English?* (second) *Which sentence would you use when talking to a friend?* (informal English)

Guide Practice
Write the following sentences on the board:

> *By combining red and blue paint, we produce purple.*
> *All passengers are to remain seated while the bus is moving.*

Ask a volunteer to rewrite the first sentence using informal language. (Sample response: *Mixing red and blue paint gives you purple.*)

Ask: *How does your choice of words change the tone of the sentence?* (may include slang, contractions) *Has the structure of the sentence changed? Is it a complete sentence or a sentence fragment? Is this acceptable in informal English?* (yes) Repeat the process with the remaining sentence.

Name_____ Date_____

Formal and Informal English

We speak and write in different ways. We speak with friends differently than with our teachers. Depending on the audience and kind of communication, we use **formal** or **informal** English.

Informal	**Formal**
It was five bucks.	It cost five dollars.
I wanna go.	I would like to go.

Read the following sentences. Rewrite each using formal English.

1. What a hit, right over the fence!

_____

_____

2. What I want to know is, who took the cookies?

_____

_____

3. The drummer, the one in front, he's very good.

_____

_____

4. First you make a left, then two blocks, go right.

_____

_____

5. Careful, the tea's steaming hot!

_____

_____

COMMON CORE
STATE STANDARD
L.4.3c

Name_____ Date_____

Formal and Informal English

Read the following examples of formal English. Rewrite each sentence in informal English.

1. Mindy purchased flowers and strawberries at the farm stand.

_____

_____

2. Please put the milk in the refrigerator while I scramble the eggs.

_____

_____

3. The family reunion will take place at the state park.

_____

_____

4. When the picture frame fell to the floor, the glass cracked.

_____

_____

5. Remember to bring pencils and erasers tomorrow for the test.

_____

_____

Lesson Plan Teacher Worksheet

Vocabulary Acquisition and Use

The lessons in this section are organized in the same order as the Common Core Language Standards for vocabulary acquisition and use. Each mini-lesson provides specific, explicit instruction for a Language standard and is followed by multiple practice pages. Use the following chart to track the standards students have practiced. You may wish to revisit mini-lessons and practice pages a second time for spiral review.

Common Core State Standard	Mini-Lessons and Practice	Page	Complete (✓)	Review (✓)
L.4.4a	Mini-Lesson 15: Use Context as a Clue to the Meaning of a Word or Phrase	74		
	Practice Pages: Use Context as a Clue to the Meaning of a Word or Phrase	75		
L.4.4b	Mini-Lesson 16: Greek and Latin Affixes and Roots	78		
	Practice Pages: Greek and Latin Affixes and Roots	79		
L.4.4c	Mini-Lesson 17: Consult Reference Materials for Pronunciation and Meaning	84		
	Practice Pages: Consult Reference Materials for Pronunciation and Meaning	85		
L.4.5a	Mini-Lesson 18: Similes and Metaphors	90		
	Practice Pages: Similes and Metaphors	91		
L.4.5b	Mini-Lesson 19: Idioms, Adages, and Proverbs	96		
	Practice Pages: Idioms, Adages, and Proverbs	97		
L.4.5c	Mini-Lesson 20: Antonyms and Synonyms	102		
	Practice Pages: Antonyms and Synonyms	103		

COMMON CORE
STATE STANDARD
L.4.4a

Use Context Clues

> **COMMON CORE STATE STANDARD L.4.4a**
> Use context (e.g., definitions, examples, or restatements in text) as a clue to the meaning of a word or phrase.

Explain

Tell students how to use context clues to determine the meaning of words.

Say: *Context clues help readers figure out the meaning of new words, words with more than one meaning, or phrases using words in a new way. A context clue can be a definition, an example, or a restatement. We can use what we already know about words or look in a dictionary or thesaurus for more information.*

Model

Write these words on the board: *apple, howled, blanket, running*. Ask students to tell you the meaning of each of these words and write the meanings next to the words. Then write the following sentences on the board, underlining the words and phrases shown:

1. *Dario is the <u>apple of his grandmother's eye</u>—even when he is acting up, she enjoys him.*
2. *The wind <u>howled</u> all night, keeping us awake with its noise.*
3. *In the morning, there was a <u>blanket</u> of new snow covering the ground.*
4. *When I left the hot water <u>running</u>, my father told me to turn it off.*

Ask students what those words mean in those sentences. Prompt them to share how they determined the meanings of these familiar words used in unfamiliar ways?

Guide Practice

Write these sentences on the board, underlining the words and phrases shown. Ask a volunteer to circle the context clue in the first sentence and tell whether it is a definition, an example, or a restatement. Then ask another volunteer to state the meaning of the underlined word.

1. *Jonas picked out several <u>garments</u>, including a jacket, a shirt, and a pair of jeans.* (example: *a jacket, a shirt, and a pair of jeans*)
2. *Elena's boat was made of <u>aluminum</u>, a kind of metal that is strong and lightweight.* (definition: *a kind of metal that is strong and lightweight*)
3. *We took our dog Roscoe to get his <u>vaccinations</u>, or shots.* (restatement: *shots*)

Have the students find the context clues in each sentence. Remind them that context clues help us figure out the meanings of words.

Name_____ Date_____

COMMON CORE
STATE STANDARD
L.4.4a

Use Context as a Clue to the Meaning of a Word or Phrase

Context clues help us figure out the meaning of new words. Context clues can be definitions, examples, or restatements in context.

- Mia sang into a <u>microphone</u>, so the audience could hear her.
- Sophie felt cold, so she pulled the <u>pashmina</u> around her shoulders.
- Dennis bought his mother some <u>stationery</u> so she could write letters to her friend.

Use the context clues in each sentence to help you understand the meaning of the underlined words. Write the meaning of each underlined word on the line.

1. The building had started to <u>decay</u>, but Robin wanted to fix it up.

   _____

2. William is the most <u>courageous</u> person I know—he saved an old woman from a burning building.

   _____

3. My cousin Ed loves to <u>tinker</u> with machines and try to make them work better.

   _____

4. It took four of us to <u>hoist</u> the heavy box onto the shelf.

   _____

5. We looked into the deep <u>gorge</u> and saw the river far below.

   _____

COMMON CORE
STATE STANDARD
L.4.4a

Name_____ Date_____

Use Context as a Clue to the Meaning of a Word

Complete each sentence by restating the underlined word in the space provided.

1. The hero of the story performed brave <u>deeds</u>, or

   _____.

2. Many <u>species</u>, or _____ of trees, make up the forest outside of Brockton.

3. For drinking, cooking, and bathing, clean water is <u>crucial</u>, or

   _____.

4. She was <u>fatigued</u>, or _____, after staying up all night to study for the test.

Use the space provided to complete the sentence with examples of the underlined word.

5. When Casey and Lin went to Spain, their <u>baggage</u> included

   _____.

6. When we went hiking, we packed plenty of <u>provisions</u> for lunch,

   such as _____.

7. The riches of the pirates' <u>plunder</u> included _____

   _____.

8. Our parents <u>forbid</u> us from doing things inside the house such as

   _____.

Name_____ Date_____

Use Context as a Clue to the Meaning of a Phrase

Use context clues to define the underlined phrases.

1. Phil's Pancake House was <u>far and away</u> the best restaurant in town.

_____

_____

2. The answer to our question is still <u>up in the air</u>, and we won't be sure until next week.

_____

_____

3. Andre <u>got a kick out of</u> hearing his younger brother tell jokes.

_____

_____

4. When Alli and Hannah were arguing, Ms. Dunn told them to <u>break it up</u> or they would have detention.

_____

_____

5. Colin has taken lessons for years and he <u>plays a mean</u> guitar.

_____

_____

6. Kim wasn't running for president anymore, so the class election was <u>up for grabs</u>.

_____

_____

COMMON CORE
STATE STANDARD

L.4.4b

Greek and Latin Affixes and Roots

COMMON CORE STATE STANDARD L.4.4b

Use common, grade-appropriate Greek and Latin affixes and roots as clues to the meaning of a word (e.g., *telegraph, photograph, autograph*).

Explain
Learning common Greek and Latin roots and affixes can help readers understand the meaning of an unfamiliar word.

Say: *Many words in the English language are based on Greek and Latin roots. Many common English prefixes and suffixes come from the Greek and Latin languages as well. Learning these word parts helps us figure out the meanings of new words as readers and helps us select and spell appropriate words as writers.*

Model
Write the following chart on the board:

Root	Origin	Meaning	English Word
aud	Latin	hear	auditorium
photo	Greek	light	photograph

Say: *If we know the meaning of the root* aud, *we understand the word* auditorium *has to do with hearing. We hear a speaker in an auditorium. We know* photo *means "light."* Graph *means "to write," so* photograph *means "light writing."*

Guide Practice
Write the following chart on the board:

Root	Origin	Meaning	English Word
phon		sound	
auto		self	
bio		life	

Ask a volunteer to write a word that includes the first root. (*phonics, telephone*)

Ask: *How does knowing the meaning of the root word help us understand the meaning of the word?* (by providing clues)
Repeat the procedure with the remaining words.

Erase the words provided by volunteers. Have students write the roots and their meanings in their notebooks, along with at least two words using each root.

Common Core Language Grade 4 • ©2014 Newmark Learning, LLC

Name_____ Date_____

COMMON CORE
STATE STANDARD
L.4.4b

Greek and Latin Affixes

Learning common **Greek and Latin affixes** can help readers understand unfamiliar words. Much of the English language is made up of words with Greek and Latin roots.

Prefix: **pre**- (before)   **pre**view, **pre**miere, **pre**dict

Suffix: -**ist** (one who)   art**ist**, dent**ist**, chem**ist**

Choose three prefixes and three suffixes from the boxes. Write a word using each prefix and suffix you have chosen. Think about what their meanings have in common.

Prefixes	
ab- (apart, away from)	inter- (between)
anti- (against)	peri- (around)
bi- (two)	post- (after)
ex- (out)	re- (back, again)

_____   _____

_____   _____

_____   _____

Suffixes	
-able (able)	-ice (condition, state, quality)
-ade (result of action)	-hood (order, condition, quality)
-an (native of)	-tion (result, state of)

_____   _____

_____   _____

_____   _____

COMMON CORE
STATE STANDARD
L.4.4b

Name_____ Date_____

Greek and Latin Affixes

Read each sentence. Circle the word that best completes the sentence. Use a dictionary if necessary.

1. The lights in the refrigerator are _____; they turn on when the door opens.

   automatic   autobiographic   autographic

2. Mom is reading a _____ about Abraham Lincoln.

   biology   biography   bionic

3. When you are on stage, remember to speak into the _____ so everyone can hear.

   microscope   microphone   microbe

4. Gemma called on the _____ to ask about our homework assignment.

   gramophone   homophone   telephone

5. Minnie gets upset when she hears _____ of her paintings or drawings.

   optimism   socialism   criticism

6. Mr. Walker stopped the _____ from riding into the street and into traffic.

   pianist   cyclist   novelist

Common Core Language Grade 4 • ©2014 Newmark Learning, LLC

Name_____ Date_____

COMMON CORE
STATE STANDARD
L.4.4b

Greek and Latin Roots

Learning common **Greek and Latin roots** can help readers understand unfamiliar words. By looking at root words, as well as the prefix or suffix of a word, we can figure out the meaning of a word we do not know.

(to speak)	dictionary	dictate	diction
(to move)	motion	motor	motivate

Circle the word that correctly completes each sentence. Use a dictionary if necessary.

1. I can't ride the merry-go-round because I feel sick when I
   _____.

   evolve   revolve   involve

2. The bakery _____ cookies from Italy.

   exports   transports   imports

3. The bird few so quickly I didn't have time to _____
   and take the photo.

   react   enact   transact

4. When Nan feels sick, her mother checks her temperature with a
   _____.

   barometer   micrometer   thermometer

5. Ben saw some penguins at the new _____.

   aquamarine   aquarium   aquanaut

COMMON CORE
STATE STANDARD
L.4.4b

Name_____ Date_____

Greek and Latin Roots

Read each Greek or Latin root. List at least two words that contain the root, using a dictionary if needed. Then write a sentence with one of the words.

1. act (do)

_____ , _____

_____

_____

2. meter (measure)

_____ , _____

_____

_____

3. aqua (water)

_____ , _____

_____

_____

4. port (carry)

_____ , _____

_____

_____

COMMON CORE
STATE STANDARD
L.4.4b

Name_____ Date_____

Greek and Latin Roots and Affixes

Choose four roots and/or affixes from the box. Write at least two words using each. Write a sentence using one word in each group.

-phon (sound)	**auto- (self)**
anti- (against)	**bio- (life)**
-ence (state of)	**-scop (see)**
-ible (can be)	**tele- (far off)**
co- (together)	**micro- (small)**

1. _____, _____

_____

_____

2. _____, _____

_____

_____

_____

3. _____, _____

_____

_____

4. _____, _____

_____

_____

Consult Reference Materials

COMMON CORE STATE STANDARD L.4.4c
Consult reference materials (e.g., dictionaries, glossaries, thesauruses), both print and digital, to find the pronunciation and determine or clarify the precise meaning of key words and phrases.

Explain
Tell students that dictionaries, glossaries, and thesauruses are three kinds of reference materials. These materials help writers spell words, understand word meanings, and find related words.

Say: *Sometimes when we write, we need to check a word's meaning or spelling. Other times, we need to see if we can find a better word to use for a certain purpose. We may need to check a word's pronunciation, or the way it is spoken, to make sure we're saying it correctly. At these times, we can use a dictionary, glossary, or thesaurus for help.*

Model
Display a dictionary entry or write the following on the board.

> *transport* (trans-port) *v.* to carry or move from one place to another; *n.* a ship or plane used to transport people or goods
>
> (from the Latin word *transportare*, meaning "to carry across")

Say: *Imagine you're writing a story about people traveling across the ocean in a ship. You want to use the word* transport *but you're not sure if that's the right word. The dictionary tells the word's meanings when the word is used as a verb or as a noun. It also shows you how to pronounce the word:* trans-port. *If you wanted to know other words with meanings similar to* transport, *you could look up the word in a thesaurus.*

Guide Practice
Write the following words on the board. Provide the students with online or print dictionaries. Work along with them to look up the first word and identify its pronunciation and meanings.

   kindergarten   *junction*   *fleet*   *envy*

Then ask students to independently find the next words and record the same information.

Name_____ Date_____

COMMON CORE
STATE STANDARD
L.4.4c

Consult Reference Materials for Pronunciation

Reference materials often have a **pronunciation key**. A pronunciation key tells how to say a word. Some words are spelled the same, but are pronounced differently.

1. *dove* (DUV) *n.* a bird   **2.** *dove* (DOVE) *v.* to jump off

A <u>dove</u> flew through the sky.   She <u>dove</u> off the diving board.

Each pair of words below are spelled the same, but pronounced differently and mean different things. Use a dictionary to find the meaning of each word. Write a sentence using each word correctly.

1. read (REED)

_____

_____

read (RED)

_____

_____

2. wind (WINED)

_____

_____

wind (WIND)

_____

_____

COMMON CORE
STATE STANDARD
L.4.4c

Name_____ Date_____

Consult Reference Materials for Pronunciation

Use a dictionary to look up the pronunciation of each underlined word. Write the pronunciation on the line provided.

1. We tried our best to be careful while we were moving Grandma's <u>delicate</u> vase.

   _____

   _____

2. Robbie had a great singing voice so we said he should join the <u>chorus</u> at school.

   _____

   _____

3. The summer evening was perfect except for the <u>mosquito</u> that kept buzzing around.

   _____

   _____

4. Looking out to the ocean, Captain Jones could see a <u>schooner</u> moving across the waves.

   _____

   _____

5. The movie was about a great <u>chemist</u> who found out how to turn wood into gold.

   _____

   _____

Name_____ Date_____

COMMON CORE
STATE STANDARD
L.4.4c

Consult Reference Materials for Meaning

Dictionaries, **glossaries**, and **thesauruses** give important information about word meanings. Dictionaries and glossaries tell what words mean, their parts of speech, and often word origins or where they came from. Thesauruses tell about words that have similar meanings.

Using a dictionary, find the answer to each question below.

1. If you have <u>agoraphobia</u>, what are you afraid of?

_____

2. If your friend said she saw a <u>cygnet</u> at the zoo, what did she see?

_____

3. Mayflies have an <u>ephemeral</u> life. What does that mean?

_____

4. If your parents said they were growing <u>frangipanis</u>, what would they be growing?

_____

Using a thesaurus, find a word that means the same as each word.

5. gumption _____

6. hullabaloo _____

7. lugubrious _____

8. quixotic _____

COMMON CORE
STATE STANDARD
L.4.4c

Name_____ Date_____

Consult Reference Materials for Meaning

Use a dictionary to find the meanings of these words.
Then, write the word that fits best on the blank space.

1. The first _____ (accent, ascent) of the high

   mountain by the explorers was a very difficult task.

2. I always _____ (counsel, council) my friends that

   they should do their homework right after school.

3. Mandy hid her diary so nobody would read her

   _____ (personal, personnel) feelings.

4. Doctor Henderson was one of the most _____

   (respectable, respective) people in our neighborhood.

5. The student's writing was so unclear that his report was almost

   _____(illegible, eligible)!

6. Before she started school, Yoko bought pens, paper, and other

   _____ (stationary, stationery) for her work.

Name_____ Date_____

COMMON CORE
STATE STANDARD
L.4.4c

Consult Reference Materials for Pronunciation and Meaning

For each problem, choose whether you should use a dictionary or thesaurus. Then, use that reference material to solve the problem.

1. Jake wants to find a word that means the same thing as *scuffle*.

   Should he use a dictionary or thesaurus? _____

   A word Jake can use is _____

   _____

2. Luis is not sure how to say the word *banquet*.

   Should he use a dictionary or thesaurus? _____

   The pronunciation of *banquet* is _____

   _____

3. Alexis wants to know if the word *cunning* is similar to the word *sly*.

   Should she use a dictionary or thesaurus? _____

   Is *cunning* similar to *sly*? _____

   _____

4. Rosa wants to know two meanings of the word *band*.

   Should she use a dictionary or thesaurus? _____

   What are two meanings of *band*? _____

   _____

COMMON CORE
STATE STANDARD
L.4.5a

Similes and Metaphors

COMMON CORE STATE STANDARD L.4.5a

Explain the meaning of simple similes and metaphors (e.g., *as pretty as a picture*) in context.

Explain

Tell students that similes and metaphors help make language more interesting.

Say: *Authors often use special techniques called figurative language to make their writing more colorful and interesting. When we read these expressions, we may have to use our imaginations to help us picture what the author means. Two types of figurative language are similes and metaphors. Explain that a simile compares two things using the word* like *or* as, *while a metaphor compares them by saying that one actually IS the other. Common similes include "strong as an ox" and "sweet as sugar."*

Model

Write these sentences on the board:

> *The kitten's fur was soft.*
> *The kitten's fur was as soft as a cloud.*
> *The kitten's fur was a pillow of feathers.*

Point out the description of the kitten's fur in the second sentence and the comparison of the fur and a pillow of feathers, two unlike things, in the third sentence.

Guide Practice

Write the following sentences on the board. Ask two volunteers to rewrite the first sentence, the first using a simile and the second using a metaphor.

> *The baby was happy.*
> (The baby was as happy as a sunbeam. The baby was a dancing sunflower.)
> *The pancakes were sweet.*
> *My mother is nice.*

Ask: *What are the clues that the first sentence is a simile? (as) How do we know the second sentence is a metaphor? (use of a "to be" verb)*

Repeat the procedure with the remaining sentences. Erase the sentences written by volunteers. Have students write the sentences in their notebooks and rewrite each using similes and metaphors. Remind them that similes and metaphors help make language more interesting.

Name_____ Date_____

Common Core
State Standard
L.4.5a

Similes

> A **simile** compares two unlike things using the words <u>like</u> or <u>as</u>. They are used to help readers make strong connections.
>
> - Speaking in public made her nervous <u>as a cat</u>.
> - This coffee is <u>as hot as the sun</u>!

Write a sentence using each of the following similes.

1. sly as a fox

_____

_____

2. jumpy as a rabbit

_____

_____

3. slow like molasses

_____

_____

4. strong as an ox

_____

_____

5. sweet like sugar

_____

_____

COMMON CORE
STATE STANDARD
L.4.5a

Name_____ Date_____

Similes

Rewrite each sentence using a simile.

1. The forest was dark.

_____

_____

2. The sky was blue.

_____

_____

3. His flower garden is colorful.

_____

_____

4. The store was crowded.

_____

_____

5. Her dress was wrinkled.

_____

_____

Name_____ Date_____

COMMON CORE
STATE STANDARD
L.4.5a

Metaphors

> **Metaphors** make direct comparisons of two unlike things, saying one actually is the other. Metaphors often use "to be" verbs instead of *like* or *as*.
>
> • It was so crowded that we <u>were tiny fish swimming in the sea</u>.
> • Her diary <u>was her best friend</u>, guarding her secrets.

Rewrite each sentence using a metaphor. Underline the two unlike things being compared.

1. Rita's boots were wet.

_____

_____

2. The cat's claws are sharp.

_____

_____

3. The playground was crowded.

_____

_____

4. Our school is large.

_____

_____

5. Gary runs quickly.

_____

_____

COMMON CORE
STATE STANDARD

L.4.5a

Name_____ Date_____

Metaphors

Rewrite each sentence using a metaphor. Underline the two unlike things being compared.

1. Mel's diary is private.

_____

_____

2. Jorge is tall.

_____

_____

3. Dad is smart.

_____

_____

4. The cheetah is swift.

_____

_____

5. The storm was noisy.

_____

_____

6. The lake was smooth.

_____

_____

Common Core Language Grade 4 • ©2014 Newmark Learning, LLC

Name_____ Date_____

COMMON CORE
STATE STANDARD
L.4.5a

Similes and Metaphors

Read the sentences below. Rewrite each sentence, first using a simile and then using a metaphor.

1. Red's basket was full.

_____

_____

2. Dana sings well.

_____

_____

3. The cherries are juicy.

_____

_____

4. The music is loud.

_____

_____

5. The trip was long.

_____

_____

COMMON CORE
STATE STANDARD
L.4.5b

Idioms, Adages, and Proverbs

> **COMMON CORE STATE STANDARD L.4.5b**
> Recognize and explain the meaning of common idioms, adages, and proverbs.

Explain

Tell students that idioms, adages, and proverbs are types of expressions and sayings that have nonliteral meanings—or meanings beyond what can be understood by individual words.

Say: *An adage is an old saying that contains a truth, like "The early bird gets the worm." A proverb, like "An apple a day keeps the doctor away," usually includes advice on how to behave. An idiom is a cultural or local expression that others may not understand. But all these expressions give information or share ideas in a quick way that is recognized by others in their culture.*

Model

Write the following sentences on the board.

1. *Don't judge a book by its cover.* (Things and people are not always what they seem.)
2. *Don't put all your eggs in one basket.* (Don't depend on just one thing.)
3. *Are you pulling my leg?* (Are you trying to fool me?)

Discuss what each expression means.

Guide Practice

Write the following expressions on the board. Ask a volunteer to explain the first expression.

A penny saved is a penny earned. (Sample response: Anything you don't spend is like money earned.)
Rome wasn't built in a day.
Don't spill the beans.

Ask: *Were you able to determine the meaning of the expression?*

Repeat the procedure with each expression. Have the students determine the meanings for the other expressions, and then ask them if they know any other proverbs, adages, or idiomatic expressions. Remind them that expressions give information or share ideas in a quick way that is recognized by others in their culture.

Name_____ Date_____

COMMON CORE
STATE STANDARD
L.4.5b

Idioms

An **idiom** is figurative language that expresses an idea through a shortcut. Idioms vary by location. Sometimes people who speak the same language do not use the same idioms. American idioms are familiar to most people in this country.

- Barking up the wrong tree
- A taste of your own medicine
- A drop in the bucket

Underline the idiom or idioms in each sentence.

1. Krysta said she would set up the library's website, but actions speak louder than words.

2. He had a rags-to-riches story, and his beautiful family was just icing on the cake.

3. After the argument, Joshua said Deshawn had a chip on his shoulder, but it takes two to tango.

4. Luke must have a cast-iron stomach, because he ate a baker's dozen of hot dogs.

5. Grace was trying to follow Madison, but Madison gave her the slip.

6. Mike stayed home from school today because he was feeling under the weather.

Name_____ Date_____

Idioms

**Read the following sentences and underline the idioms.
Then explain what each idiom means.**

1. Timmy was already crying, and when Alicia knocked down his
tower of blocks it just added fuel to the fire.

_____

_____

2. It was raining cats and dogs when we got to the baseball field, so
we couldn't play.

_____

_____

3. We tried to keep Chanda's party a secret, but Eldon spilled the
beans.

_____

_____

4. "Hold your horses, Mike," said the coach. "It's only halftime, so
keep your chin up."

_____

_____

5. Jose hit the nail on the head when he said the problem was with
the committee.

_____

_____

Common Core Language Grade 4 • ©2014 Newmark Learning, LLC

Name_____ Date_____

COMMON CORE
STATE STANDARD
L.4.5b

Adages and Proverbs

> **Adages and proverbs** are familiar sayings that have been part of languages for a long time. Adages are simply old sayings, while proverbs are old sayings that give advice. Some sayings could be considered either a proverb or an adage, because the two are similar.
>
> Beauty is only skin deep. (adage)
> Absence makes the heart grow fonder. (adage)
> Practice makes perfect. (proverb)
> When in Rome, do as the Romans do. (proverb)

Underline the adage or proverb in each sentence.

1. "Vijay, don't hit Samir back," Ms. Bridges said. "Two wrongs don't make a right."

2. When Mom finally sat down to her knitting, Grandma said, "A man's work is from sun to sun, but a woman's work is never done."

3. "Well of course she wanted a favor in return," said Cali. "There's no such thing as a free lunch."

4. "Please wear your helmet when you ride your bike," said Dad. "An ounce of prevention is worth a pound of cure."

5. "You might win the contest," said Mom, "but don't count your chickens before they hatch."

COMMON CORE
STATE STANDARD
L.4.5b

Name_____ Date_____

Adages and Proverbs

Write a sentence using each of the following proverbs or adages. Make sure your sentence helps the reader understand the proverb or adage.

1. All work and no play makes Jack a dull boy.

_____

_____

2. A journey of a thousand miles starts with a single step.

_____

_____

3. Words can cut like a knife.

_____

_____

4. Make hay while the sun shines.

_____

_____

5. A bird in the hand is worth two in the bush.

_____

_____

Common Core Language Grade 4 • ©2014 Newmark Learning, LLC

Name_____ Date_____

Idioms, Adages, and Proverbs

Underline three examples of an idiom, adage, or proverb in the passage below. Then write what each expression means on the lines below.

Henry woke up, trudged down the stairs, and sat at the end of the table. His cereal was waiting for him. With a frown on his face, he poked at it with his spoon. "Someone woke up on the wrong side of the bed this morning," said Mom.

"I just want my new bike to get here," said Henry with a pout.

"A watched pot never boils," said Mom, "Go play outside. I'm sure it will arrive soon."

Henry got up and walked to the front door. He saw Dad pulling his truck into the driveway. "Hey bud," said Dad, "Got something for you. It cost me an arm and a leg!" He pulled a brand new blue bicycle out of the trunk.

"Wow!" yelled Henry, running over to the bike. "Thanks, Dad!"

1. _____

_____

2. _____

_____

3. _____

_____

COMMON CORE
STATE STANDARD

L.4.5c

Antonyms and Synonyms

> **COMMON CORE STATE STANDARD L.4.5c**
> Demonstrate understanding of words by relating them to their
> opposites (antonyms) and to words with similar but not identical
> meanings (synonyms).

Explain

Tell students that antonyms and synonyms are used to help us figure out the
meaning of new words.

Say: *Synonyms are words with similar, but not identical meanings. Antonyms
are words with opposite meanings. The similar and opposite meanings that
writers add to their sentences help readers picture and understand what new
words mean. As writers, we can include synonyms and antonyms as context
clues for our readers. We can use information from a dictionary or thesaurus
as well as what we already know about words to help us use these clues in
writing.*

Model

Write these words on the board:

> *boisterous* (loud, quiet)
> *cackle* (laugh, cry)

Ask the students to write a synonym and an antonym for each word. Point out
that the word *boisterous* means nearly the same thing as the word *loud* and
the opposite of the word *quiet*. Point out that the word *cackle* means nearly
the same thing as the word *laugh* and the opposite of the word *cry*.

Guide Practice

Write these words on the board. Ask a volunteer to write at least one synonym
and one antonym for each word.

1. *tasty* (synonyms: *delicious, yummy, divine*; antonyms: *tasteless, yucky,
   gross*)
2. *cold* (synonyms: *freezing, icy, frigid*; antonyms: *warm, hot, scorching*)
3. *brave* (synonyms: *courageous, strong, fearless*; antonyms: *fearful,
   cowardly, scared*)

Repeat the procedure with each word. Then have the students think of other
synonyms and antonyms for each word.

Name_____ Date_____

COMMON CORE
STATE STANDARD
L.4.5c

Antonyms

> **Antonyms** are words that have opposite meanings.
>
> - agree, disagree   • happy, sad
> - tired, energetic   • upset, calm

Choose the correct antonym from the box to complete each sentence.

vivid	bulky	cautious	bitter	coordinated

1. Jill is clumsy and drops things, while Barry is

_____.

2. Phil is _____, but his brother Brett
is careless.

3. Grandma likes oranges because they are sweet, but she does not

like lemons because they are _____.

4. The old photo looked blurry, but the painting was

_____.

5. Her old coat felt too _____, while

her new coat felt light.

COMMON CORE
STATE STANDARD
L.4.5c

Name_____ Date_____

Antonyms

Write an antonym for each word below.

1. enormous _____

2. add _____

3. sob _____

4. reckless _____

5. terrible _____

6. waddle _____

7. thankful _____

8. nervous _____

9. wobble _____

10. thrifty _____

11. exhausted _____

12. interesting _____

COMMON CORE
STATE STANDARD
L.4.5c

Name_____ Date_____

Synonyms

Synonyms are words that have similar meanings.

- strong, muscular   • nuisance, pest
- sweet, sugary   • smile, grin

Choose a synonym from the box to replace the underlined word in each sentence.

squabble	crunched	sleepy	bugs	excited

1. Mom said she felt <u>tired</u> after working later at work.

   _____

2. Marjorie was <u>delighted</u> that her best friend Joanie was in her

   Spanish class. _____

3. The students learned about <u>insects</u> in biology class.

   _____

4. My brother and I <u>argue</u> a lot. _____

5. The horse <u>chewed</u> the apple loudly. _____

COMMON CORE
STATE STANDARD
L.4.5c

Name_____ Date_____

Synonyms

Circle the synonyms in each set of words.

1. nibble   prepare   race   make

2. none   some   zero   lots

3. airplane   train   car   automobile

4. furniture   giraffe   garments   clothing

5. jump   dance   slouch   leap

6. boring   awkward   uneasy   normal

7. furious   jealous   angry   discouraged

8. thin   large   petite   hefty

9. explore   perfect   plain   investigate

10. lawn   mound   grass   highway

11. construct   simple   build   demolish

12. manage   control   release   ignore

Name_____ Date_____

COMMON CORE
STATE STANDARD
L.4.5c

Antonyms and Synonyms

An analogy is a comparison between two things that have something in common. Select the correct word to complete each analogy and tell whether the words are antonyms or synonyms in the space provided.

1. **Lake** is to **river** as **forest** is to _____.

   (jungle, playground, kingdom)

   Antonyms or synonyms? _____

2. **Praise** is to **criticize** as **energetic** is to _____.

   (sloppy, dishonest, fatigued)

   Antonyms or synonyms? _____

3. **Groan** is to **wail** as **anxious** is to _____.

   (ashamed, cruel, troubled)

   Antonyms or synonyms? _____

4. **Shallow** is to **deep** as **dim** is to _____.

   (brilliant, determined, recent)

   Antonyms or synonyms? _____

5. **Least** is to **fewest** as **hungry** is to _____.

   (gloomy, starving, lonesome)

   Antonyms or synonyms? _____

How to Use the Practice Assessments

The quick practice assessments provided in this section are designed for easy implementation in any classroom. They can be used in several different ways. You may wish to administer a conventions assessment and a vocabulary assessment together. They may also be used individually as an informal assessment tool throughout the year. Use the following charts for item analysis and scoring.

Student Name:

Conventions	Date	Item	Standard	✔=0 X=1	Total
Assessment 1		1	**L.4.2a:** Use correct capitalization.		
		2	**L.4.2b:** Use commas and quotation marks to mark direct speech and quotations from a text.		
		3	**L.4.1d:** Order adjectives within sentences according to conventional patterns.		
		4	**L.4.1g:** Correctly use frequently confused words.		
		5	**L.4.1c:** Use modal auxiliaries to convey various conditions.		
		6	**L.4.1f:** Produce complete sentences, recognizing and correcting inappropriate fragments and run-ons.		
Assessment 2		1	**L.4.2d:** Spell grade-appropriate words correctly, consulting references as needed.		
		2	**L.4.1g:** Correctly use frequently confused words.		
		3	**L.4.2a:** Use correct capitalization.		
		4	**L.4.1g:** Correctly use frequently confused words.		
		5	**L.4.2d:** Spell grade-appropriate words correctly, consulting references as needed.		

Student Name:

Conventions	Date	Item	Standard	✓=0 X=1	Total
Assessment 3		1	**L.4.1f:** Produce complete sentences, recognizing and correcting inappropriate fragments and run-ons.		
		2	**L.4.1e:** Form and use prepositional phrases.		
		3	**L.4.2d:** Spell grade-appropriate words correctly, consulting references as needed.		
		4	**L.4.1g:** Correctly use frequently confused words.		
Assessment 4		1	**L.4.1g:** Correctly use frequently confused words.		
		2	**L.4.1g:** Correctly use frequently confused words.		
		3	**L.4.2b:** Use commas and quotation marks to mark direct speech and quotations from a text.		
		4	**L.4.1f:** Produce complete sentences, recognizing and correcting inappropriate fragments and run-ons.		
		5	**L.4.1f:** Produce complete sentences, recognizing and correcting inappropriate fragments and run-ons.		
Assessment 5		1	**L.4.1a:** Use relative pronouns (*who, whose, whom, which, that*) and relative adverbs (*where, when, why*).		
		2	**L.4.2a:** Use correct capitalization.		
		3	**L.4.2d:** Spell grade-appropriate words correctly, consulting references as needed.		
		4	**L.4.1b:** Form and use the progressive (e.g., *I was walking; I am walking; I will be walking*) verb tenses.		
		5	**L.4.1d** Order adjectives within sentences according to conventional patterns.		

Student Name:

Vocabulary	Date	Item	Standard	✔=0 X=1	Total
Assessment 1		1	**L.4.4c:** Consult reference materials, both print and digital, to find the pronunciation and determine or clarify the precise meaning of key words and phrases.		
		2	**L.4.4c:** Consult reference materials, both print and digital, to find the pronunciation and determine or clarify the precise meaning of key words and phrases.		
		3	**L.4.4a:** Use context (e.g., definitions, examples, or restatements in text) as a clue to the meaning of a word or phrase.		
		4	**L.4.4a:** Use context (e.g., definitions, examples, or restatements in text) as a clue to the meaning of a word or phrase.		
		5	**L.4.4c:** Consult reference materials, both print and digital, to find the pronunciation and determine or clarify the precise meaning of key words and phrases.		
		6	**L.4.4c:** Consult reference materials, both print and digital, to find the pronunciation and determine or clarify the precise meaning of key words and phrases.		
Assessment 2		1	**L.4.4c:** Consult reference materials, both print and digital, to find the pronunciation and determine or clarify the precise meaning of key words and phrases.		
		2	**L.4.4c:** Consult reference materials, both print and digital, to find the pronunciation and determine or clarify the precise meaning of key words and phrases.		
		3	**L.4.4c:** Consult reference materials, both print and digital, to find the pronunciation and determine or clarify the precise meaning of key words and phrases.		
		4	**L.4.4c:** Consult reference materials, both print and digital, to find the pronunciation and determine or clarify the precise meaning of key words and phrases.		
		5	**L.4.4c:** Consult reference materials, both print and digital, to find the pronunciation and determine or clarify the precise meaning of key words and phrases.		

Common Core Language Grade 4 • ©2014 Newmark Learning, LLC

Student Name:

Vocabulary	Date	Item	Standard	✔=0 X=1	Total
Assessment 3		1	**L.4.5b:** Recognize and explain the meaning of common idioms, adages, and proverbs.		
		2	**L.4.5b:** Recognize and explain the meaning of common idioms, adages, and proverbs.		
		3	**L.4.5b:** Recognize and explain the meaning of common idioms, adages, and proverbs.		
		4	**L.4.5b:** Recognize and explain the meaning of common idioms, adages, and proverbs.		
Assessment 4		1	**L.4.4a:** Use context (e.g., definitions, examples, or restatements in text) as a clue to the meaning of a word or phrase.		
		2	**L.4.6:** Acquire and use accurately grade-appropriate general academic and domain-specific words and phrases, including those that signal precise actions, emotions, or states of being and that are basic to a particular topic.		
		3	**L.4.4a:** Use context (e.g., definitions, examples, or restatements in text) as a clue to the meaning of a word or phrase. **L.4.6:** Acquire and use accurately grade-appropriate general academic and domain-specific words and phrases, including those that signal precise actions, emotions, or states of being and that are basic to a particular topic.		
		4	**L.4.4a:** Use context (e.g., definitions, examples, or restatements in text) as a clue to the meaning of a word or phrase.		
		5	**L.4.6:** Acquire and use accurately grade-appropriate general academic and domain-specific words and phrases, including those that signal precise actions, emotions, or states of being and that are basic to a particular topic.		
Assessment 5		1	**L.4.4b:** Use common, grade-appropriate Greek and Latin affixes and roots as clues to the meaning of a word.		
		2	**L.4.4a:** Use context (e.g., definitions, examples, or restatements in text) as a clue to the meaning of a word or phrase.		
		3	**L.4.4b:** Use common, grade-appropriate Greek and Latin affixes and roots as clues to the meaning of a word.		
		4	**L.4.4a:** Use context (e.g., definitions, examples, or restatements in text) as a clue to the meaning of a word or phrase.		
		5	**L.4.4a:** Use context (e.g., definitions, examples, or restatements in text) as a clue to the meaning of a word or phrase.		

COMMON CORE
STATE STANDARDS

L.4.1–
L.4.3

Name_____ Date_____

Read the passage. Then choose the correct form of the underlined sentence.

¹ <u>Kamal just got back from a trip to visit his aunt in new mexico.</u>

² <u>"I did something I've never done before", he told his best friend Justin.</u> "Aunt Roz took me to a truly special place. ³ <u>We drove in her red big car, the one that has the loud horn and the bright paint.</u> Anyway, we parked in the parking lot, and we walked to this special place." Justin listened closely. Kamal went on. "I had my camera, but ⁴ <u>I didn't know if we'd be allowed to take pitchers there.</u> Then I saw a sign that explained people had permission to take photos." Kamal pointed out that he told his aunt, ⁵ <u>"Yes, we couldn't take photos here."</u>

Justin still didn't understand what was so special about the trip. Then Kamal explained. "We walked to Four Corners. In seconds, I walked in four states! ⁶ <u>I walked in Arizona, New Mexico, Utah, and Colorado, all four states meet at Four Corners.</u> This was the best trip ever!"

1. Ⓐ kamal just got back from a trip to visit his Aunt in new mexico.

    Ⓑ Kamal just got back from a trip to visit his aunt in New Mexico.

    Ⓒ kamal just got back from a trip to visit his aunt in new mexico.

    Ⓓ no change

Name_____ Date_____

2. Ⓐ "I did something I've never done before," he told his best friend Justin.

Ⓑ "I did something I've never done before" he told his best friend Justin.

Ⓒ "I did something I've never done before, he told his best friend Justin.

Ⓓ no change

3. Ⓐ We drove in big her red car, the one that has the loud horn and the bright paint.

Ⓑ We drove in her big red car, the one that has the loud horn and the bright paint.

Ⓒ We drove in big red her car, the one that has the loud horn and the bright paint.

Ⓓ no change

4. Ⓐ I didn't know if we'd be allowed to take pictures their.

Ⓑ I didn't no if we'd be aloud to take pitchers they're.

Ⓒ I didn't know if we'd be allowed to take pictures there.

Ⓓ no change

5. Ⓐ "Yes, we may take photos here."

Ⓑ "Yes, we might take photos here."

Ⓒ "Yes, we might can take photos here."

Ⓓ no change

6. Ⓐ I walked in Arizona, New Mexico, Utah, and Colorado all four states, meet at Four Corners.

Ⓑ I walked in Arizona, New Mexico, Utah, and Colorado all four states meet at Four Corners.

Ⓒ I walked in Arizona, New Mexico, Utah, and Colorado. All four states meet at Four Corners.

Ⓓ no change

COMMON CORE
STATE STANDARDS
L.4.1–
L.4.3

Name_____ Date_____

Read the passage. Then choose the correct form of the underlined sentence.

Mica completed the research for his report on the Constitutional Convention. [1] He carefully rote the information for each of his sources, and he decided which quotes he would include. He thought about the most powerful way to begin the report. [2] He decided to begin with a quote taken from an important document. [3] He chose a quote from the Preamble to the United states constitution. Mica began his report by writing, "We the People of the United States, in order to form a more perfect union . . . "

Mica had thought a great deal about those words during his research. [4] He recognized they're importance. He realized that the Constitution was meant to include all the people forming the new nation. [5] He knew this new goverment had been the beginning of a great countrie.

Name_____ Date_____

COMMON CORE
STATE STANDARDS
L.4.1–
L.4.3

1. Ⓐ He carefully wrote the information for each of his sources and, he decided which quotes he would include.

   Ⓑ He carefully rote the information for each of his sources, and he decided which quotes he would include.

   Ⓒ He carefully wrote the information for each of his sources, and he decided which quotes he would include.

   Ⓓ no change

2. Ⓐ He decided too begin with a quote taken from an important document.

   Ⓑ He decided two begin with a quote taken from an important document.

   Ⓒ He decideed to begin with a quote taken from an important document.

   Ⓓ no change

3. Ⓐ He chose a Quote from the Preamble to the United states constitution.

   Ⓑ He chose a quote from the Preamble to the United States Constitution.

   Ⓒ He chose a quote from the Preamble to the united states Constitution.

   Ⓓ no change

4. Ⓐ He recognized there importance.

   Ⓑ He recognized their importance.

   Ⓒ He recognized theire importance.

   Ⓓ no change

5. Ⓐ He knew this new government had been the beginning of a great countrie.

   Ⓑ He knew this new goverment had been the beginning of a great country.

   Ⓒ He knew this new government had been the beginning of a great country.

   Ⓓ no change

Common Core
State Standards
L.4.1–
L.4.3

Name_____ Date_____

Read the passage. Then choose the correct form of the underlined sentence.

¹ Presentations made Dana nervous, she would chew her lip and sweat when she thought about standing in front of the class. ² That's why her upcoming presentation within volcanoes was the only thing on her mind.

³ Dana's teacher told students to listen carefuly while he gave them an exampul of a strong way to begin a presentation. He said, "Volcanoes are all over. I mean, they are so cool. Volcanoes are awesome, and I like the huge ones best." The teacher explained that students could use the right kind of language to set the tone for the rest of the presentation. The teacher went on to give more good information. He said, "Use words that best express exactly what you mean. When you describe the sound of a volcano when it erupts, use a word such as booming. ⁴ You're presentations will be stronger when you use language that tells exactly what you mean."

COMMON CORE
STATE STANDARDS

L.4.1–

L.4.3

Name_____ Date_____

1. Ⓐ Presentations made Dana nervous. She would chew her lip and sweat when she thought about standing in front of the class.

Ⓑ Presentations made Dana nervous she would chew her lip and sweat when she thought about standing in front of the class.

Ⓒ Presentations made Dana nervous she would, chew her lip and sweat when she thought about standing in front of the class.

Ⓓ no change

2. Ⓐ That's why her upcoming presentation above volcanoes was the only thing on her mind.

Ⓑ That's why her upcoming presentation around volcanoes was the only thing on her mind.

Ⓒ That's why her upcoming presentation about volcanoes was the only thing on her mind.

Ⓓ no change

3. Ⓐ Dana's teacher told students to lissen carefuly while he gave them an exampul of a strong way to begin a presentation.

Ⓑ Dana's teacher told students to listen carefully while he gave them an exampul of a strong way to begin a presentation.

Ⓒ Dana's teacher told students to listen carefully while he gave them an example of a strong way to begin a presentation.

Ⓓ no change

4. Ⓐ Your presentations will be stronger when you use language that tells exactly what you mean.

Ⓑ Youre presentations will be stronger when you use language that tells exactly what you mean.

Ⓒ Your'e presentations will be stronger when you use language that tells exactly what you mean.

Ⓓ no change

COMMON CORE
STATE STANDARDS
L.4.1–
L.4.3

Name_____ Date_____

Read this passage with errors. Rewrite the passage to fix the errors.

Chris and Gary worked with students in they're class to begin an experiment. Each student prepared to plant two flowers. Students wrote there names on two flowerpots. They wrote the letter A on one and the letter B on the other. The dirt was dry and hard. The teacher said "It's time to do the next step. You have permission to go to the sink. You can now drip water into the dirt."

Gary completed the step, he then gently slipped the roots of a tiny flower into each pot and packed dirt around the roots. The teacher said, "Measure the height of each flower. Then put flower A on the windowsill, and put flower B into the closet." Students listened closely. The teacher explained, "You have just begun. You were working on this experiment for the next three weeks. You will be recording each flower's growth. Then you will discuss the results of the experiment."

Name_____ Date_____

COMMON CORE
STATE STANDARDS
**L.4.1–
L.4.3**

_____

_____

_____

_____

_____

_____

_____

_____

_____

_____

_____

_____

COMMON CORE
STATE STANDARDS
L.4.1–
L.4.3

Name_____ Date_____

Read this passage with errors. Rewrite the passage to fix the errors.

Iman searched the Internet for biography ideas. She knew she needed to write about a person which had reached important goals, and she wanted to write about a topic she found really interesting. She decided to research astronauts. When she discovered information about Dr. mae Jemison, she knew she'd found the subject for her biography.

Iman checked owt books from the library. In one of the books, she read these two sentences: "Dr. Jemison traveled around the world to give health care to people in need. Then she became an astronaut.

Iman couldn't wait to read on and learn more. These were great two accomplishments. As Iman learned more about Dr. Jemison, she discovered something she hadn't known before. Iman was interested in becoming a doctor but she was also interested in becoming an astronaut. She'd never realized she might be able to do both.

Common Core Language Grade 4 • ©2014 Newmark Learning, LLC

COMMON CORE
STATE STANDARDS
L.4.1–
L.4.3

Name_____ Date_____

_____

_____

_____

_____

_____

_____

_____

_____

_____

_____

_____

_____

COMMON CORE
STATE STANDARDS
L.4.4–
L.4.6

Name_____ Date_____

Read the dictionary entry. Then use it to answer the questions that follow.

cur • rent (ˈkər-ənt)

n. 1. body of water or air moving in a definite direction; 2. flow of electricity; 3. general course of events. adj. 1. belonging to the present time; 2. being used commonly.

fo • cus (ˈfō-kəs)

n. 1. a clear goal; 2. the center of a person's interest; 3. the exact place where an earthquake starts. v. 1. to look closely; 2. to pay close attention to.

1. Which of these words would appear before **current** in the dictionary?

Ⓐ customer

Ⓑ cute

Ⓒ curiosity

Ⓓ curve

2. Which part of the dictionary entry above best shows how to pronounce the word **current**?

Ⓐ current

Ⓑ n.

Ⓒ adj.

Ⓓ (ˈkər-ənt)

Name_____ Date_____

3. **Read the sentence.**

The strong ocean **current** *pushed the shells toward the shore.*
Which meaning of **current** is correct in the sentence?

Ⓐ body of water or air moving in a definite direction

Ⓑ flow of electricity

Ⓒ belonging to the present time

Ⓓ being used commonly

4. Which sentence includes the word **current** used as an adjective?

Ⓐ Jeans are very popular in the current style of dress.

Ⓑ Surfers followed the current as they rode the sea waves.

Ⓒ The current moved through the wires and lit the light bulb.

Ⓓ She explained facts about current to her science class.

5. Which of these words would appear after **focus** in the dictionary?

Ⓐ fob

Ⓑ foam

Ⓒ focal

Ⓓ fodder

6. Which sentence includes the word **focus** used as a verb?

Ⓐ Finishing his homework before dinner was his focus.

Ⓑ The focus of the earthquake was far away in the ocean.

Ⓒ She focused on the movie, not saying a single word.

Ⓓ My teacher was the focus of attention in every class.

COMMON CORE
STATE STANDARDS
L.4.4–
L.4.6

Name_____ Date_____

Read the thesaurus entry. Then use it to answer the questions that follow.

> **difficult** adj. hard, demanding, burdensome, not easy.
>
> ANTONYM easy.
>
> **peculiar** adj. strange, odd, weird, puzzling.
>
> ANTONYM ordinary.

1. Which word would appear before the word **difficult** in a thesaurus?

   Ⓐ dignity

   Ⓑ dictionary

   Ⓒ direct

   Ⓓ disappointment

2. What part of speech is the word **difficult**?

   Ⓐ adjective

   Ⓑ adverb

   Ⓒ noun

   Ⓓ verb

COMMON CORE
STATE STANDARDS
L.4.4–
L.4.6

Name_____ Date_____

3. Which word has the opposite meaning of the word **difficult**?

Ⓐ burdensome

Ⓑ demanding

Ⓒ easy

Ⓓ hard

4. **Read the sentences below.**

Finishing the research was a **difficult** task. I knew some of the resources would be **difficult** to find, and I knew others would be **difficult** to read. It was clear that **difficult** work would be in my future.

What is the most likely reason the writer of these sentences would use a thesaurus to find the word **difficult**?

Ⓐ to locate the word difficult and its definition

Ⓑ to search for an antonym for the word difficult

Ⓒ to avoid repetition of the word difficult

Ⓓ to discover the part of speech of the word difficult

5. What is another antonym for the word **peculiar**?

Ⓐ extraordinary

Ⓑ regular

Ⓒ funny

Ⓓ spooky

COMMON CORE
STATE STANDARDS
L.4.4–
L.4.6

Name_____ Date_____

Read the passage. Then answer the questions that follow.

Snow blew into tall drifts outside. Maria shook her head. "How could this happen the day before the big play?" she asked her mom. "We've been practicing for months. I've never worked so hard in my life. If this storm doesn't stop, we'll be up a creek without a paddle. We won't be able to leave the house."

Maria's mom patted her on the back. "We can't control the weather," she said. "Let's just watch to see what happens. In the meantime, why don't you get your things ready tonight?"

Maria didn't budge. She was glued to her spot at the window. "Why bother?" she asked. "They'll probably just cancel the play."

"It's better to be safe than sorry," said Mom. "We might be able to go in the morning."

Maria grumbled as she plodded to her room. She prepared everything she'd need, just in case.

The next morning, sunlight streamed into Maria's room. As she opened her eyes, her mom called, "Hurry up, Maria, it's time to go!"

"What do you mean?" asked Maria.

"The snow is melting." Her mom smiled. "It's time to get this show on the road!"

Common Core Language Grade 4 • ©2014 Newmark Learning, LLC

Name_____ Date_____

COMMON CORE
STATE STANDARDS
L.4.4–
L.4.6

1. *What does the phrase "up a creek without a paddle" mean?*

Ⓐ in a body of water without a boat

Ⓑ in a condition without help

Ⓒ with swimmers in a contest

Ⓓ with friends on an island

2. What does the phrase "glued to her spot" mean?

Ⓐ She had spilled paste, and she couldn't move.

Ⓑ She was worried, and she wanted to stay where she was.

Ⓒ She had a craft project to finish, and she should keep working.

Ⓓ She had changed her mind about doing the play, and she decided to watch the snow.

3. What does the phrase "it's better to be safe than sorry" mean?

Ⓐ When things work out differently than you expect, you might find that you are unhappy and upset.

Ⓑ You should follow rules to protect yourself, especially when there is a big storm.

Ⓒ It's a good idea to make preparations, even when you think something might fail to work out.

Ⓓ People who care about you will help you work things out, but you might wish you had handled things yourself.

4. What does the phrase "it's time to get this show on the road" mean?

Ⓐ The play is starting.

Ⓑ They should leave.

Ⓒ The clock shows that it is getting late.

Ⓓ The snow should be cleared from the streets.

COMMON CORE
STATE STANDARDS
L.4.4–
L.4.6

Name_____ Date_____

Read the passage. Then answer the questions that follow.

Viewing rainbows might be a matter of beauty, but the way they form is a matter of science. Rain results in millions of water droplets forming in the air. Sunlight shines through these droplets. The light rays bend and separate. These bent light rays cause the colors that people see in a rainbow. These colors are red, orange, yellow, green, blue, **indigo**, and violet.

A rainbow is actually a circle, but people see only half of this circle, an **arc**. Why? The horizon interferes with the view. It stops people from seeing the entire circle. The horizon is a line where the earth and sky appear to meet.

Could you walk under a rainbow? **Experts agree that you could not.** When you see a rainbow, the sunlight is shining from a location behind you. When you see your shadow, this is the direction you should look as you try to find a rainbow.

What are some other places you might see rainbows? You might see them in lawn sprinklers or waterfalls.

1. Which word is the opposite of **straight** and helps the reader understand the movement of light rays?

Ⓐ millions

Ⓑ bent

Ⓒ entire

Ⓓ lawn

COMMON CORE
STATE STANDARDS
L.4.4–
L.4.6

Name_____ Date_____

2. Which answer choice lists only words and phrases that students would likely read and study while learning about the science behind rainbows?

Ⓐ beauty, people, half, usually see, people

Ⓑ line, walk under, direction, location, shadow

Ⓒ water droplets, separate, colors, arc, horizon

Ⓓ same, places, them, lawn sprinklers, waterfalls

3. Based on the passage, the reader can tell that **indigo** is a—

Ⓐ color

Ⓑ view

Ⓒ location

Ⓓ shadow

4. Based on information in the passage, what is an **arc**?

Ⓐ the direction to look to find a rainbow

Ⓑ half a circle

Ⓒ the place where the earth and sky appear to meet

Ⓓ droplets in the air

5. Which best explains what happens when experts disagree?

Ⓐ They have exactly the same ideas.

Ⓑ They have ideas that are similar.

Ⓒ They have different ideas.

Ⓓ They have ideas they found on the Internet.

COMMON CORE
STATE STANDARDS
L.4.4–
L.4.6

Name_____ Date_____

Read the passage. Then answer the questions that follow.

We often think of **communication** as happening only through words, but people can communicate in many different ways. People can communicate through symbols and signals. They can communicate through hand gestures. They can even communicate through special lights.

With so many words to express ideas, why do people need other ways to communicate? These **methods**, or ways, of communication can be useful in noisy **environments**. They can show information to people at a distance or help people figure out information quickly.

Some road signs include symbols without words. A symbol is a picture that stands for something. For example, there are signs that show students crossing the street. There are signs that show curves in a road. There are signs showing that a railroad track is near. Drivers can quickly see important information without taking the time to read many words on these signs.

The next time you think about communication, think about the many ways to communicate. Remember that people often communicate without using a single word.

Name_____ Date_____

1. Knowing that the word **communicate** means "to tell information" helps the reader understand that the word **communication** means—

Ⓐ not sharing information

Ⓑ the act of sharing information

Ⓒ a person who shares information

Ⓓ surroundings

2. Based on information in the passage, the reader can tell that the opposite of *communicating with words* is *communicating with*—

Ⓐ gestures

Ⓑ people

Ⓒ ideas

Ⓓ drivers

3. Which definition most closely defines the word **environments**?

Ⓐ airports

Ⓑ places where animals live

Ⓒ areas where plants grow

Ⓓ surroundings

4. Which word has almost the same meaning as **methods**?

Ⓐ ways

Ⓑ signs

Ⓒ express

Ⓓ information

5. A picture that stands for something is a _____.

Ⓐ distance

Ⓑ word

Ⓒ track

Ⓓ symbol

Answer Key, pages 7–14

page 7

1. who   2. that   3. which
4. whose   5. whom

page 8

1. The crab, which crawled slowly across the beach, was shaped like a horseshoe.
2. Mauri took her boot with a broken heel to a cobbler, who is a person who repairs shoes.
3. The delivery truck driver lost the package that I was expecting to receive today.
4. The rabbit, which was brown, burrowed into the ground to hide from the hot sun.
5. The teacher, whom I had been waiting for all morning, has finally arrived.
6. A plantain is a fruit that is similar to a banana.
7. The toddler, who was barely three years old, could recite the entire alphabet.
8. Carin looked up the meaning of the word *mechanical* in the dictionary, which is a book used to find the definitions of words.
9. The jury handed the envelope to the judge, who immediately opened it.
10. I have a classmate whose mother is a famous model.

page 9

1. when   2. where   3. when
4. where   5. why   6. where

page 10

1. where   2. why   3. when

(page 10 continued)

4. why   5. where   6. when
7. why   8. where   9. where
10. when

page 11

1. The vegetables, which are in the bag, need to be put in the refrigerator.
2. This is the playground that I like to play at in the summer.
3. He is a soccer player, who is also a kicker on the football team.
4. April was the month when Philip was born.
5. Not getting enough sunlight is the reason why the plant turned brown.
6. Autumn is when the leaves turn brilliant colors.
7. Paris is the place where the Eiffel Tower stands.
8. The restaurant where we ate dinner is right around the corner.

page 13

(sample answers shown)

1. Sara was jumping.
2. They were walking.
3. He was leaving.
4. The dog was behaving until her owner came home.
5. He was chewing gum when he got it stuck in his hair.
6. Rob was earning money as a salesman.

page 14

1. was collecting   2. was listening
3. were singing   4. was pedaling

Answer Key, pages 14–25

(page 14 continued)

5. was speaking   6. were working

7. was barking   8. were rehearsing

9. were studying   10. was shining

page 15

1. am sleeping   2. is watching

3. are playing   4. is baking

5. is crawling   6. are painting

page 16
(sample answers shown)

1. I am studying for my exam.

2. She is limping after breaking her leg.

3. Cindy is delivering cookies.

4. I am borrowing a book.

5. We are spying on my sister.

6. He is shutting the door behind him.

page 17

1. will be celebrating

2. will be wiggling

3. will be stalling

4. will be mopping

5. will be fading

6. will be pausing

page 18
(sample answers shown)

1. She will be worrying until the test is over.

2. It will be flooding because of the rain.

3. Beth will be teaching next week.

4. They will be deciding where to move.

5. I will be earning money tomorrow.

6. The author will be signing books.

page 19

Past Progressive: has been making, have been helping

Present Progressive: are visiting, am sewing, is making

Future Progressive: will be offering, will have made

page 21

1. would   2. must   3. might

4. will   5. should   6. can't

7. may   8. would

page 22

1. should   2. will   3. must

4. may   5. would   6. could

7. can   8. might   9. must

10. should

page 23

(sample answers shown)

1. I can ride a bike.

2. We could go to the park.

3. Would you eat dinner with me?

4. May I have a cookie?

5. Alice might follow the rabbit.

6. We must not be late!

7. You should make a decision.

8. They will win.

page 25

1. tiny, old   2. friendly, Canadian

3. tasty, red   4. colorful, plastic

5. shiny, metal

Answer Key, pages 26–35

page 26

1. a   2. b   3. b   4. a   5. a

page 27

(sample answers shown)

1. scary, horror
2. new, history
3. young, talented
4. red, juicy
5. satisfying, long
6. ancient, gold
7. wool, winter
8. cuddly, old
9. cool, blue
10. dedicated, hardworking

page 29

Marta and June studied the book <u>on Marta's desk</u>. The photos <u>of science projects</u> seemed easy, but Marta was worried <u>about the science fair</u>. June began writing <u>in her notebook</u>. She made lists <u>of things they had and things they needed</u>. "I think it will be okay," June said <u>with sympathy</u> as she wrote. Marta's last building project <u>for school</u> had been a disaster. She remembered <u>with embarrassment</u> the way her volcano had crumbled and landed <u>on the floor</u>. <u>Instead of giving up</u>, this time she would work <u>with June</u> and make a great project <u>over the weekend</u>.

Answers will vary.

page 30

(sample answers shown)

1. This puzzle piece goes above that one.
2. Let's swim across the pond.
3. She is from New Zealand.
4. The coffee is on the shelf.
5. It's water under the bridge.
6. Grab your coat before you leave.

page 31

(sample answers shown)

1. Katrina raced her brother down the street.
2. Greg hid his sister's book under his bed.
3. Would you like lunch in the park?
4. Tomas and Jamal shouted at their friends.
5. The yellow bird swooped through the trees.
6. Mom's friends visited in the summer.
7. My grandparents enjoyed touring the museum during the day.
8. The rain fell in the ditch.

page 33

Complete sentences: 1, 4, 7, 8, 9

page 34

(sample answers shown)

1. Marcia and Ellen are sisters.
2. After the movie, we had dinner.
3. We searched everywhere before we found the book.
4. My neighbor's dog is annoying.
5. When we opened the door, a surprise was waiting for us.
6. As the wind began to blow, the house began to shake.
7. The lightning almost hit me!
8. We sang songs in the car until we arrived at the movie theater.

page 35

1. The smallest kitten in the box made the most noise.

Answer Key, pages 35–43

(page 35 continued)

2. It was very dark. Marcus and Gerry were sure they heard a noise coming from the next room.

3. When the wind picked up, the leaves scattered across the yard and caught in the fence.

4. The girls followed the rabbit they saw in the park to see where it was going.

5. A ball of yarn rolled across the floor after I knocked over the basket.

6. Mother enjoys seeing the daffodils blooming in her garden in April.

page 36

1. Molly had to change her shoes. They were wet from the rain.

2. Dad writes everything on his calendar. He hates to forget about basketball games.

3. Would you like some hot soup? It will warm you up.

4. Tomas carried his skateboard up the hill because it was too steep to ride.

5. The baby laughed when she saw the butterfly. She cried when it flew away.

6. It was raining hard; Ms. Walker closed her fruit stand and went home.

page 37

Ladybug beetles are very useful in the garden. They eat insects such as aphids, which eat plants. Ladybugs protect our plants by eating these pests. Ladybugs don't have to worry too much about being eaten when they're at work in the garden. Their red wings warn birds to stay away because ladybugs taste terrible. Ladybugs have another defense, too. They can release liquid that tastes bad from their legs.

page 39

(sample answers shown)

1. My grandma is such a dear.

2. We often have deer in our yard.

3. My hair is so short!

4. A hare is similar to a rabbit.

5. It's your turn to drive.

6. That is its favorite spot to sleep.

page 40

1. I	2. bee	3. hear
4. they're	5. plain	6. were
7. close	8. herd	

(sample answers shown)

9. I broke my <u>right</u> hand.

10. She likes to <u>write</u> stories.

page 41

(sample answers shown)

1. You're just pulling my leg.

2. This is your penguin.

3. Do you know the answer?

4. When is the homework due?

5. The Tigers won the game!

6. One is the loneliest number.

7. I see you over there.

8. The sea can be treacherous.

page 43

1. <u>Boy Scouts, Mexico</u>

2. <u>Arbor Day, Mrs. Gibbons</u>

3. <u>Slice of Pizza Pizzeria, Falls Boulevard</u>

4. <u>Ernesto, Berkeley College, English</u>

5. <u>Roba's Farm, October</u>

6. <u>Batman, Halloween</u>

Answer Key, pages 43–51

(page 43 continued)

7. French, Spanish

8. Nightmare Before Christmas

9. Russia, Moscow

10. Italy, Spain, Mediterranean Sea

page 44

1. Randy and Rex live on 231 Thompson Street in the town of Hillshire.

2. My favorite book is *Freckle Juice* by Judy Blume.

3. My sister Marilyn attends the University of Pennsylvania, where she studies Spanish and French.

4. On Tuesday, May 5, 2005, I visited the Empire State Building in New York City.

5. Reggie buys used books at a store called Almost New, which is located on Main Street near Peggy Sue's Deli.

page 45

(sample answers shown)

1. Maple Lane
2. Atlantic Ocean
3. Michael
4. Boston
5. Marta
6. Canada
7. Idaho
8. *Finding Nemo*
9. Memorial Day
10. Saturn

page 47

1. "Oh, I can carry it," the child said cheerfully. "It isn't heavy."

2. "Mine is a long and a sad tale!" said Mouse, turning to Alice.

3. "Which direction should I go?" she asked.

4. "I don't see," said Caterpillar.

5. "By the powers, Ben Gunn!" roared Silver.

page 48

1. "When will he come home, Marmee?" asked Beth, with a little quiver.

2. Alice crawled into the chair, sighing, "This has been quite a day."

3. "Goodness, just look at the time!" cried Nancy as she rose to her feet.

4. "Hannah, please pour a glass of water for Mrs. Ritter," suggested Carla.

5. "Don't mind me. I'm as happy as a cricket here," answered Jo.

page 49

1. Rachel said, "I will buy milk after I return my library books."

2. "What time is practice?" Tomas asked.

3. "Stop! Wait for me!" Liz shouted to the bus driver.

4. "I saw a sea lion when I visited the aquarium Saturday," said Kim.

5. "Wear a hat this morning. It's cold!" insisted Mom.

page 50

1. Aristotle once said, "A friend to all is a friend to none."

2. "The only way to have a friend is to be one," said Ralph Waldo Emerson.

3. "Try not to become a man of success," said Albert Einstein, "but rather try to become a man of value."

4. According to Woody Allen, "Eighty percent of success is showing up."

page 51

1. "Honesty is the first chapter in the book of wisdom," said President Thomas Jefferson.

2. According to the poet Robert Frost, "A poem begins in delight and ends in wisdom."

Answer Key, pages 51–57

(page 51 continued)

3. President John F. Kennedy once said, "A child miseducated is a child lost."

4. "All that I am, or hope to be," said President Abraham Lincoln, "I owe to my angel mother."

5. Playwright William Shakespeare wrote, "The course of true love never did run smooth."

page 52

1. "The time to repair the roof is when the sun is shining," said President John F. Kennedy.

2. According to Confucius, "Life is really simple, but we insist on making it complicated."

3. William Shakespeare wrote, "Love all, trust a few, do wrong to none."

4. "Alone we can do so little; together we can do so much," stated Helen Keller.

5. "I know that I am intelligent," said Socrates, "because I know that I know nothing."

page 53

Ms. Martinez sat down next to her daughter, Rosie, on the bench. "What's the score?" she asked, looking across the field.

"Three to five," Rosie answered. Rosie played soccer, too. She wanted to get better, so she watched a lot of good teams play. She hoped to learn some of their skills.

Rosie blinked. "I heard someone talking about something Yogi Berra said, and I decided he had the right idea."

"What did Yogi Berra say?" her mother asked.

"You can observe a lot by watching." Rosie grinned.

page 55

1. Kim is bringing a tent, and Roger will help to set it up.

2. It didn't rain yesterday, nor did it rain last night.

3. Tammy may read a magazine, or she may read a book.

4. The roses are beautiful, but my sister prefers daisies.

5. The sun is shining, yet we feel very cold.

page 56

Jenna and Ricardo both have brothers, but their brothers are very different. Jenna's brother, Paul, likes to run, so he joined the school track team. Paul wins a lot of races, yet he's very humble. Ricardo's brother, Tomas, likes to cook, so he makes dinner for his family on Sundays. Tomas can make vegetable soup, and he can make pancakes. Jenna and Ricardo could learn from their brothers, yet they have never asked Paul and Tomas to teach them new skills.

page 57

1. My sister likes yogurt, but she's allergic to dairy foods.

2. We were out of bananas, so we went to the market.

3. Miguel has a new skateboard, yet he prefers to ride the old one.

4. You may do your homework at your desk, or you may take it to the library.

5. Vic won't eat tomatoes, nor will he eat squash.

6. Mom is painting the living room, for the wallpaper is old and faded.

Answer Key, pages 59–65

page 59

curious, frightening, elephant, creature

page 60

1. spectacular　　2. spectacle

3. speculate　　4. spectator

page 61

Answers may vary.

page 63

(sample answers shown)

I was <u>astonished</u> when my Uncle Jake said I had to <u>invent</u> an <u>original frozen yogurt</u> flavor for his <u>awesome</u> shop, <u>Tenth Avenue Yogurt Factory</u>. He wanted something <u>extreme</u> that kids in my school would <u>gobble up</u> and then <u>come back for more</u>. He already had some <u>crazy</u> flavors, like sweet potato cashew and french fry and ketchup. My <u>mission</u> was to take yogurt to <u>infinity and beyond</u>. I <u>jumped</u> into the project with a list of foods I see kids eating at lunch time. The first <u>two</u> on the list were peanut butter and mac and cheese. I also <u>recalled</u> that my best friend Eli puts peanut butter on his grilled cheese sandwiches and <u>insists</u> that it's <u>delicious</u>. I spent <u>four</u> days making lists and thinking and talking to my classmates. Then I told Uncle Jake what the <u>brand-new</u> flavor must be: peanut butter with mac and cheese.

page 64

(sample answers shown)

1. Christine's spirited horse won both one-mile races at the annual rodeo.

2. Matt's chocolate cake was quickly eaten up at the Fourth of July celebration at the county courthouse.

(page 64 continued)

3. The noisy bus climbed the steep hill on a stormy afternoon.

4. My favorite cousin Gino goes hiking on the narrow trails that weave up the rocky hills behind his house.

5. Becky likes pepperoni pizza, especially the kind from the Italian shop over in the local mall.

6. Bella usually does her homework during class.

7. After the teacher finished explaining the assignment, Tommy carefully started working on his essay.

8. Tristan went to the front of the room and nervously waited for his turn to play.

9. At the zoo, we saw two cheetahs playfully running after a toy.

10. Katie unwillingly shared her raisin bun with her sister.

page 65

(sample answers shown)

1. Marianne borrowed her mother's car and carefully drove to Farrell's Department Store on Mason Street.

2. Sweat dripping from his face, Kamal leaped back onto the stage thrashing his battered acoustic guitar.

3. Louis collapsed onto his bed without changing his clothes and was snoring in less than a minute.

4. Aunt Carolyn stretched out comfortably on her favorite lounge chair and opened her new novel.

5. Grandfather took little Elsa to buy a pair of pink winter boots and found a good pair of work boots for himself, too.

Answer Key, pages 65–76

(page 65 continued)

6. Jennifer visited the shelter three times before she decided on Roxy, the shiny black Labrador retriever.

page 67

(sample answers shown)

1. That was Mike—the guy from the hardware store.

2. I have an appointment with the doctor tomorrow (I think).

3. "Please take me to school," said Beth.

4. Wow! That is amazing!

page 68

1. c   2. a   3. b   4. a   5. c

page 69

1. I told Juan (at least I thought I did) that the party is tonight.

2. We caught three kinds of fish (trout, bluegills, and bass) at the lake on Saturday.

3. Did you get a letter—the one from school—today?

4. Jack is kind, funny, and dependable—he is my best friend.

5. "The contest winners," said Keesha, "are Winston and Nelson."

6. "Don't you dare touch my teddy bear!" yelled my little sister.

page 71

(sample answers shown)

1. The player hit the ball, which went over the fence.

2. I want to know who took the cookies.

3. The drummer in front is very good.

(page 71 continued)

4. First turn left, then go two blocks and turn right.

5. Be careful; the tea is very hot.

page 72

(sample answers shown)

1. Mindy got flowers and strawberries from the farm stand.

2. Put the milk away please, while I make eggs.

3. We'll have the reunion at the park.

4. The picture frame hit the floor and cracked.

5. Don't forget pencils and erasers for the test tomorrow.

page 75

(sample answers shown)

1. weaken or rot

2. brave, daring, bold

3. fool around, play, fix

4. lift, raise

5. valley, canyon

page 76

(sample answers shown)

1. acts

2. kinds, types

3. necessary, key, important

4. tired, sleepy, weary

5. suitcases, bags, backpacks

6. sandwiches, drinks, fruit, food

Answer Key, pages 76–88

(page 76 continued)

7. gold, coins, jewels

8. screaming, yelling, running

page 77

(sample answers shown)

1. by far, easily

2. uncertain, undecided

3. enjoyed, liked

4. stop, end it

5. plays well

6. open, unfilled

page 79

(sample answers shown)

Prefixes:

absent, antidote, bicycle, exterior, interlibrary, periscope, postscript, rewrite

Suffixes:

agreeable, blockade, American, justice, neighborhood, prevention

page 80

1. automatic
2. biography
3. microphone
4. telephone
5. criticism
6. cyclist

page 81

1. revolve
2. imports
3. react
4. thermometer
5. aquarium

page 82

(sample answers shown)

1. actor, reactor; He is a great actor.

(page 82 continued)

2. thermometer, kilometer; The thermometer read below freezing.

3. aquatic, aquarium; We toured the aquarium.

4. airport, teleport; The airport closed during the storm.

page 83

Answers may vary.

page 85

(sample answers shown)

1. I read three books every week. Last month she read five books.

2. Please wind the clock. The wind blew through the trees.

page 86

Style of pronunciations will vary based on the reference material that is used by students.

page 87

1. crowded places; enclosed spaces
2. a young swan
3. very short-lived
4. tropical tree
5. initiative, sense, spirit
6. fuss, commotion, upoar
7. gloomy, sad, unhappy
8. idealistic, romantic, unrealistic

page 88

1. ascent
2. counsel
3. personal
4. respectable
5. illegible
6. stationery

Answer Key, pages 89–98

page 94

page 89

(sample answers shown)

1. thesaurus, fight
2. dictionary, bang-kwit
3. thesaurus, yes
4. dictionary, a stripe or a musical group

page 91

(sample answers shown)

1. The crafty cat was sly as a fox.
2. After the soccer game, Ed was jumpy as a rabbit.
3. Walking home, Gina was slow like molasses.
4. The firefighter was strong as an ox.
5. The fresh apples are sweet like sugar.

page 92

(sample answers shown)

1. The forest was dark as a closet.
2. The sky was as blue as a jellybean.
3. His flower garden is like a box of crayons.
4. The store was like a swarm of ants.
5. Her dress was like the skin on an elephant's knees.

page 93

(sample answers shown)

1. Rita's <u>boots</u> were <u>sponges</u>.
2. The cat's <u>claws</u> are <u>fishing hooks</u>.
3. The <u>playground</u> was a <u>jungle</u> of wild creatures.
4. Our <u>school</u> is a giant <u>maze</u> of hallways.
5. <u>Gary</u> is a <u>gazelle</u> on the plains.

page 94

(sample answers shown)

1. Her <u>diary</u> is a best <u>friend</u> who keeps secrets.
2. <u>Jorge</u> is a *towering* <u>redwood</u>.
3. <u>Dad</u> is an <u>encyclopedia</u>.
4. The <u>cheetah</u> is a <u>tornado</u> *streaking* across the plains.
5. The <u>storm</u> was a freight <u>train</u>, bearing down on us.
6. The <u>lake</u> was a <u>mirror</u> reflecting the clear sky.

page 95

(sample answers shown)

1. Red's basket was like an overflowing cornucopia. Red's basket was a bursting sack.
2. Dana sings like a lark. Dana's singing is heaven.
3. The cherries are like bursting water balloons. The cherries are geysers of flavor.
4. The music is like thunder. The music is a screaming crowd.
5. The trip was as long as a lifetime. The trip was a lifelong journey.

page 97

1. *actions speak louder than words*
2. *rags-to-riches, icing on the cake*
3. *chip on his shoulder, it takes two to tango*
4. *cast-iron stomach, baker's dozen*
5. *gave her the slip*
6. *under the weather*

page 98

1. *added fuel to the fire;* made things worse

Answer Key, pages 98–106

(page 98 continued)

2. raining cats and dogs; raining hard

3. *spilled the beans*; told the secret

4. *Hold your horses*; be patient. *Keep your chin up*; stay hopeful

5. *hit the nail on the head*; got it exactly right

page 99

1. *Two wrongs don't make a right.*

2. *A man's work is from sun to sun, but a woman's work is never done.*

3. *There's no such thing as a free lunch.*

4. *An ounce of prevention is worth a pound of cure.*

5. *Don't count your chickens before they hatch.*

page 100

(sample answers shown)

1. Stan was happy to be going on vacation—all work and no play makes Jack a dull boy.

2. I started the quilt by cutting the fabric into squares; after all, a journey of a thousand miles starts with a single step.

3. Jenny really hurt my feelings, because words can cut like a knife.

4. Everything was ready and I had the day off, so I decided to make hay while the sun shines.

5. Mom didn't get me the radio I really wanted, but a bird in the hand is worth two in the bush.

page 101

1. wrong side of the bed—to awake grouchily or in a bad mood

(page 101 continued)

2. A watched pot never boils—time takes longer when you're waiting for something to happen.

3. an arm and a leg—a large amount of money

page 103

1. coordinated   2. cautious

3. bitter   4. vivid

5. bulky

page 104

(sample answers shown)

1. tiny   2. subtract

3. laugh   4. responsible

5. awesome   6. run

7. ungrateful 8. relaxed

9. steady   10. generous

11. awake   12. boring

page 105

1. sleepy   2. excited

3. bugs   4. squabble

5. crunched

page 106

1. prepare, make

2. none, zero

3. automobile, car

4. garments, clothing

5. jump, leap

6. awkward, uneasy

7. furious, angry

8. large, hefty

Answer Key, pages 106—121

(page 106 continued)

9. explore, investigate

10. lawn, grass

11. construct, build

12. manage, control

page 107

1. jungle, synonyms

2. fatigued, antonyms

3. troubled, synonyms

4. brilliant, antonyms

5. starving, synonyms

Assessment Section:

pages 112–113

1. B	2. A	3. B
4. C	5. A	6. C

pages 114–115

1. C	2. D
3. B	4. B
5. C	

pages 116–117

1. A	2. C
3. C	4. A

pages 118–119

Chris and Gary worked with students in <u>their</u> class to begin an experiment. Each student prepared to plant two flowers. Students wrote <u>their name</u> on two flowerpots. They wrote the letter A on one and the letter B on the other. The dirt was dry and hard. The teacher <u>said,</u> <u>"It's</u> time to do the next step. You have permission to go to the sink. You can now drip water into the dirt."

(pages 118–119 continued)

Gary completed the <u>step. He</u> then gently slipped the roots of a tiny flower into each pot and packed dirt around the roots. The teacher said, "Measure the height of each flower. Then put flower A on the windowsill, and put flower B into the closet." Students listened closely. The teacher explained, "You have just begun. You <u>will be</u> working on this experiment for the next three weeks. You will be recording each flower's growth. Then you will discuss the results of the experiment."

pages 120–121

Iman searched the Internet for biography ideas. She knew she needed to write about <u>a person who had</u> reached important goals, and she wanted to write about a topic she found really interesting. She decided to research astronauts. When she discovered information about <u>Dr. Mae Jemison</u>, she knew she'd found the subject for her biography.

Iman <u>checked out books</u> from the library. In one of the books, she read these two sentences: "Dr. Jemison traveled around the world to give health care to people in need. Then she became <u>an astronaut."</u>

Iman couldn't wait to read on and learn more. These were <u>two great</u> accomplishments. As Iman learned more about Dr. Jemison, she discovered something she hadn't known before. Iman was interested in becoming a <u>doctor, but</u> she was also interested in becoming an astronaut. She'd never realized she might be able to do both.

Answer Key, pages 122—131

pages 122–123

1. C	2. D
3. A	4. A
5. D	6. C

pages 124–125

1. B	2. A
3. C	4. C
5. B	

pages 126–127

1. B	2. B
3. C	4. B

pages 128–129

1. B	2. C
3. A	4. B
5. C	

pages 130–131

1. B	2. A
3. D	4. A
5. D	

Common Core Language Grade 4 • ©2014 Newmark Learning, LLC